Crystal Doorways

Simon & Sue Lilly

Crystal Doorways

ISBN 1 898307 98 9

Cover design by Paul Mason

Published by:

Capall Bann Publishing
Freshfields
Chieveley
Berks
RG20 8TF

Contents

Preface

This book is not another volume telling you everything you wanted to know about crystals and crystal healing! "*Crystal Doorways*" focuses on a very particular system of using crystals and colour to bring about changes in your consciousness and an increased understanding of the energy-world around us.

Whether you use the suggestions in this book as a way of simply having a change from everyday reality (without giving yourself a hangover or worse!), or whether you use the information to help with healing, we are sure you will have a lot of fun.

The idea of using an arrangement of crystals placed on and around the body has been known for a long time. These patterns are often called "layouts" or "grids". Whilst there were useful suggestions for layouts in crystal books written in the 1970's and 1980's, many required a vast number of large, expensive crystals or an honours degree in geometry to work them out - that is after you'd managed to translate the text out of metaphysical gobbledygook into everyday English.

It was Sue who first experimented with using small, easily obtainable crystals in simple arrangements to see what effect they might have. The "amethyst healing net" (see page 107), was the first to be discovered. Several years later Sue and Simon met whilst working at a school teaching colour healing, and during a period of intensive training developed a system for identifying specific patterns that would tune a person's awareness to a particular band of energy vibration. This is when the term "energy net" was born. "Grid" was a popular word at the time, and smacked of electricity cables and rigidity. On the whole, the use of semi-technical language when talking about crystals and subtle energies may be of some use to explain a concept, but the terms too easily become accepted, not as an analogy, but as an actuality. This is when misunderstandings begin to proliferate at an alarming rate as assumptions breed further assumptions. This text is full of ideas, some of them you may agree with, some you may not. Too much is accepted as truth just because it is in print. Please take what is of use to you here and leave the rest for later!

All around the country, at talks, seminars and in our own training courses for the last couple of years, we have demonstrated energy nets and have been constantly surprised at the immediacy and clarity of the system. We rarely give people any clues as to what they are likely to experience and yet their reports, more often than not, fall into recognisable patterns. Even the hardened sceptic will occasionally surprise themselves!

You will find each energy net illustrated and described in full with what stones to use, where to place them, what the net can be used for and some background information that you may find useful. If you are a complete newcomer to crystal work we suggest you start off with the amethyst healing net and then gradually try out some others.

Finally, although energy nets are simple and usually only need small tumbled stones, they can be extremely powerful. Please be sure to read and follow the guidelines for use!

Exminster, Devon
June, 1996

Introduction

Whenever we are talking about the nature of subtle energies and their effects on physical reality it is important to remember that the concept of solid matter is extremely subjective. To quote Ra Bonewitz: " *If the nucleus of an average atom were the size of a tennis ball, the electron would be smaller than a grain of sand, and the outermost would be circling at a distance of four miles*" ('*Cosmic Crystals*')

Nature of crystals

A lot has been said about the spiritual and healing qualities of crystals in the last couple of decades. Much personal exploration, if not subjective experience, has gone on and often appears to conflict with others who are in the same field. However, the tangible, measurable physical properties of crystals alone make them worthy of investigation.

The mineral kingdom is the physical basis for all evolutionary growth. That is to say, all forms of life on this planet have evolved directly because of the particular proportion of minerals available in the earth's crust. The mineral kingdom is the raw material, the building blocks and the foundation for all life-forms with physical bodies.

Every mineral will form crystals if the environment is favourable. Under the right conditions of temperature and pressure, in a liquid or gaseous medium with sufficient raw materials, atoms and molecules attract each other and will arrange themselves in a regular lattice, a three-dimensional repeating pattern in which each atom finds the most stable relationship possible with its neighbours. Once formed, because of the nature of each crystal's structure, they are the most stable, constant matter in creation.

It is this regularity of pattern which establishes the precise geometrical form of crystals - the outside harmony is simply a reflection of the internal structure. Without one the other would not be possible.

If a mineral shows geometrical form it is a crystal of that mineral and has the most orderly possible arrangement of atoms for that substance. No matter how a crystal looks - whether it is clear or not etc. etc., the fact that it exists in that form means it has inherent orderliness and harmony.

The industrial and technological uses for crystals rely on their property of orderliness and the fact that when subjected to any form of stress, be that pressure, heat or electricity, the atoms will adjust in some way so as to return as quickly as possible to their stable resting state. The adjustment takes the form of a slight expansion of size, a release of electric charge, light, and so on, which is then used.

The relationship of crystal systems to the human system

A look at the difference between a crystal system and the human system on the physical levels gives some ideas of how and why crystals have profound effects.

A crystal is one chemical compound and nothing else. It has inherent orderliness and the ability to adjust to changes in its environment. It has inherent stability and at the vibrational level will maintain a constant electromagnetic pattern.

The human body, on the other hand, is composed of hundreds of thousands of different compounds, some elementary, some simple and some composed of hundreds of different molecules. Every molecule has its own vibratory signature and its own interactions with the environment.

The unit of the physical body, the cell, contains DNA and RNA each with thousands of molecules as well as other proteins, enzymes, internal structures and organelles. Each component has differing electrical charges and biomagnetic fields, and each goes to make up increasingly large and complex systems.

The following analogy can be used to describe the potential effects of a crystal coming into the bioelectromagnetic field of the body.

Imagine the body as an enormous orchestra with millions of instruments (vibrational rates) using the same basic score (DNA) but following different parts (the function of cell, organ, system), playing without stopping for fifty, sixty, seventy years.

Over time we could imagine some players giving up altogether, some getting bored and changing the notes they use, some getting out of tune and others losing their place or reading someone else's part. Essentially, when the body picks up stress (some outside influence good or bad, which alters the functioning of the whole system), it is like one instrument going slightly off key or falling behind by a note or two - a disharmony enters the system. The more disharmony there is, the harder it gets for the remaining instruments to stick to the score in front of them. Into this potential cacophony of vibrational rates, bringing a crystal is like striking a tuning fork. One single, pure tone is constantly emitted with no change, no variation, and this acts as a guide by which a retuning can occur that reasserts local harmony.

From another viewpoint, because the same basic constituents are present throughout the universe, the energies contained within the crystal forms are also universal and all-pervading. Crystals reflect the basic harmonies of matter which could be called the fundamental laws of nature. Any state of disharmony is due to an imbalance of the natural laws and using crystals can potentially give access to those energies we require.

Crystal nets - how they work

The skin of the physical body is not where the individual stops. Even within orthodox non-quantum science many outer levels are recognised. There is the thermal layer, similar to the planet's atmosphere and beyond that (as well as interpenetrating the physical), there is a complex electromagnetic field which is a product of the functions of the physical body, and which also controls and regulates the system.

It is by means of this bioelectromagnetic body that we are in contact with our local environment and with the electromagnetic field of the planet itself.

In terms of energy fields we are a localised pattern that remains coherent for a certain period of time (a lifetime), within a much larger field of energy (the planet), which in its turn is a localised field in the sun's vast electromagnetic sea which is localised within the galaxy, and so on. There are a multitude of types of energy that impinge on our body awareness that rarely emerge into conscious awareness. Nonetheless they are ever-present and modify our behaviour patterns.

The way the body is organised links its perceptive ability to certain energy bands (those we call sound, visible light and so on). If we were able to change our own bioelectromagnetic pattern in some way it would be possible to link our personal pattern to a slightly different pervading universal pattern, thus altering our experience and perceptions.

This is what happens inside an energy net. Each crystal modifies the body's energy relationship to its environment and allows access to other layers of information.

Each crystal's inherent energy pattern is amplified and/or modified by its relationship to the stones around it. The whole pattern creates a window of energy that modifies, replaces or negates the day-to-day patterns of the body to the planet and solar system. The crystal net is potentially so powerful because the coherence of energy within each stone can act as an override to the less organised or more general fields around it.

An energy net can allow a reharmonising of some aspect of the physical system; or can create, recreate or bring to awareness the energy of a different part of the solar system or universe;or if there is a pattern that is perceived as negative or life-damaging in some way, an emotion or illness or other sort of disease,an energy net can impose a stronger harmonising pattern to disrupt and de-structure the negative pattern.

We are awash in a galactic ocean of energy patterns. Depending on where we are in the ocean we perceive and are effected by different currents and tides and live alongside different sorts of beings. A crystal net does what it says:each one is particularly organised to "catch" one type of energy. All energy is omnipresent and all-pervasive, it requires only the correct "bait" to find it.

The nature of patterns

All pattern and all geometry springs from a point that neither has mass nor form. This is the "bindu" of Vedic thought: the "point-limit", the finest, subtlest event when the universal becomes particular - where "thingness", and so duality, arises. Space arises when the point moves - a line initiates the first dimension. The succeeding dimensions are created as the first dimension line moves its position relative to the first point, becoming two and then three dimensional.

In three dimensions the point can be seen as a sphere (that is, a point with mass) and the way these points/spheres fit together in space is the basis for all form, all geometry and all the shapes and structures of matter. Thus pattern and number are so fundamental to existence that nothing is more important. The relationship of points in space IS what matter is about. The exterior shapes we see in crystals are merely the most obvious expression of the inevitable patterning of all matter whether it be organic or inorganic.

We are using a language here derived from Greek thought on the "measuring of the Earth" (geometry) with all its "hedra" beginning with tetrahedra, through cubes and evolving into the complexity of solid form. We could equally chose to describe the same process of manifestation in terms of the creation of deities from an originating principle or manifestation condensing as the sephira sephiroth. Number is another symbolic representation of the patterns that space and matter create.

Whenever we deal with shape or number - with anything more than "one" - we are setting up a rhythm of patterns. This patterning creates an energy resonance, like ripples on a pool, with all the other patterns of that type. For example, setting up three points in relation to each other creates a triangle. Three points create the energy tension between them and set up a resonant field that we call a "triangle". This triangle will resonate with "threeness" and triangularity throughout creation.

Such disciplines as numerology, gematria and geomancy draw their rationale from this perception of the importance of pattern. Where they may tend to fall short in popular usage, is the ability to recognise significant pattern resonances. As all time, space and matter is essentially the relationship of form and number it is hardly difficult to make something fit into any number of patterns. Choosing the most significant resonant pattern is therefore the skill necessary.

Such skill was applied in the creation of sacred buildings throughout the world. Whether pyramid, stone circle or temple, each was a preconceived, or perhaps intuitive understanding of geometry to capture (or create) the essence of form and initiate a tangible and continuous vibration or resonance of energy within their structures.

We ourselves have become so pre-fabricated to cubic consciousness that it may take some time to un-cube our resonance and be able to recognise the more complex and certainly more powerful energies that echo within other types of built space.

Putting crystals, with their primal geometric purity, in a geometric relation to each other - so giving one a set of energy patterns an even larger, overlying energy pattern - is going to create quite a resonant vibration. This is likely to be a particularly strong experience to someone inside the web of symbolic and actual energies. But what can happen if we were to work with just space itself?

Experimenting with simple two-dimensional geometrical form is an eye-opening experience. You will never walk on a patterned carpet or a tiled floor with the same awareness again!

Using thin card draw and cut out a triangle, or several types of triangle - i.e. equilateral, isoceles, scalene, large enough to comfortably stand on so your feet don't poke out over the edges. Take a minute or two to just stand on the floor (unpatterned if possible) and tune in to how your body feels. Then stand on the cut-out shape and take a moment or two to see if you feel any different. Have a go at making some other shapes: square, hexagon, decagon, circle, random curvy shape, random jagged shape.

Move from one to the other fairly quickly and note how you feel on each. After doing this you will know a little of what it must be like to have a flying carpet.

Subjective experience will differ but there will be correlations and what is important, is that most people will have definite, different experience on different shapes - sometimes a physical or balance sensation, sometimes a sense of movement or stability, sometimes a change of mood. And this is just consciously standing on "a bit of shaped cardboard"!

To take the experiment a little further, use string or ribbon and pins to mark out larger areas of geometric shape, large enough to sit or lie in - no crystals, no colour - nothing seemingly powerful at all - except marked out lines in two-dimensional space. You can get a bit more ambitious and intersect different forms - interpenetrate triangles, diamonds, create simple yantra or mandala forms. You will find, even when the line drawing is not exactly geometrically correct, that each shape or pattern will give a very different experience as if each is a doorway to a different world. (Of course you may use the even more intangible chalk lines if you have a suitable floor and you don't mind being known as a sorcerer!)

Matter builds up geometrical pattern and creates us humans. Our brains are designed, our senses are attuned, to recognising and utilising pattern. Chaos (non-order) is where there is a failure to recognise any pattern - no point of reference, no point or sphere of stability, nothing falls into relationship with anything else - no point! Where we find we have a lack of orderliness in our lives (usually it is not chaos but a pattern of such complexity we can't grasp it) - we can be helped by installing ourselves within a strong resonant pattern. An energy net using colour, crystal and number can give us that point of reference, a new perspective, a breathing space, a time of clarity from which to re-establish our own identity, our own resonance with creation.

The science of ritual - the combination of the senses

In the West we tend to be suspicious of ritual and uncomfortably nervous if we have to take part in one. Ritual is seen as superstitious, unscientific, childish, pretend, superficial. Our understanding of ritual is as misplaced and shallow as our understanding of play. Play is something children do before they grow out of it and start to live a useful life of work in the "real world".

From the outside ritual is nonsensical theatre. It may even appear that way from the inside too. This is because, like play, ritual suspends our knowledge of how the world usually is and how it usually works.

The purpose of ritual and play is to establish a new set of rules for reality and then to work through them to their natural conclusion. Play is a way of exploring one's potential in a non-threatening situation. Ritual is a way of stepping into a new set of rules to reach some reality not easily available or accessible to everyday experience, but that will somehow create change in the "real world".

Both play and ritual "work" when we suspend our everyday judgement and dive into the possibility presented by the new rules. Ritual can be achingly complex, minutely detailed and the results can be mindblowingly powerful, or ritual can be simple, fluid and elegant and still be mindblowingly powerful. This is because ritual is a science, a "knowing".

What ritual knows is that to shift consciousness, to alter perceptions, to change reality as experienced, it is necessary to activate more than just the surface mind of rational thought and endless chatter. The more of the whole mind that can be entranced, excited and stimulated, the greater the ability to shift consciousness.

Ordinary language, the language of our mental chatter, exists to identify everyday patterns, everyday things, from the perspective of here-and-now reality. Ordinary language cannot easily go beyond these boundaries because of the built-in limitations of function. Non-verbal means of communication, whether it be through movement, sound, smell, taste, touch or sight, activate deeper, less restricted areas of the brain and have an immediate effect on the whole of brain functioning. Ritual talks to the whole-mind in the language it can understand best.

Our senses are the only link we have to the world outside us. Usually our senses are directed in such a way as to remind us where and when we are at all times during our waking moments. If we can direct what we experience on the level of all the senses in a very particular way then our "where and when" feedback, our everyday mental chatter, fades into the background and new states of awareness and new experiences are more likely to occur.

In its simplest form, ritual creates a new space in which we can experience a non-ordinary reality. It can be as basic as turning off the 'phone and lighting a candle. Following the "guidelines for using nets" presented here can be done in a ritually aware manner and this will help to make the best use of time spent within the energy net.

An important part of the procedure of crystal nets is the use of background colour. Not only does a coloured cloth have a specific effect on the physical, mental and emotional system via the eyes, but it also sets up a background vibration (the energy that we recognise as "colour"), which is in harmony with the more precise orientation of the gemstones and amplifies their action.

It would be possible to tune the other senses as well by using an appropriate incense or essential oil; lighting candles of a particular colour or scent; playing or listening to music; chanting or otherwise calling in energies, god-forms and other beings to be present. Suggested correspondences can be found in the Appendices, but please experiment with your own ideas and sense of appropriate play. Get used to what each net feels like before adding other elements to the procedure.It will probably be best not to clutter the experience within the net with too much sensory overload - give yourself some quietness to experience what is actually going on! Try introducing different ritual elements before entering the net experience itself, and see which enhance and which reduce your awareness.

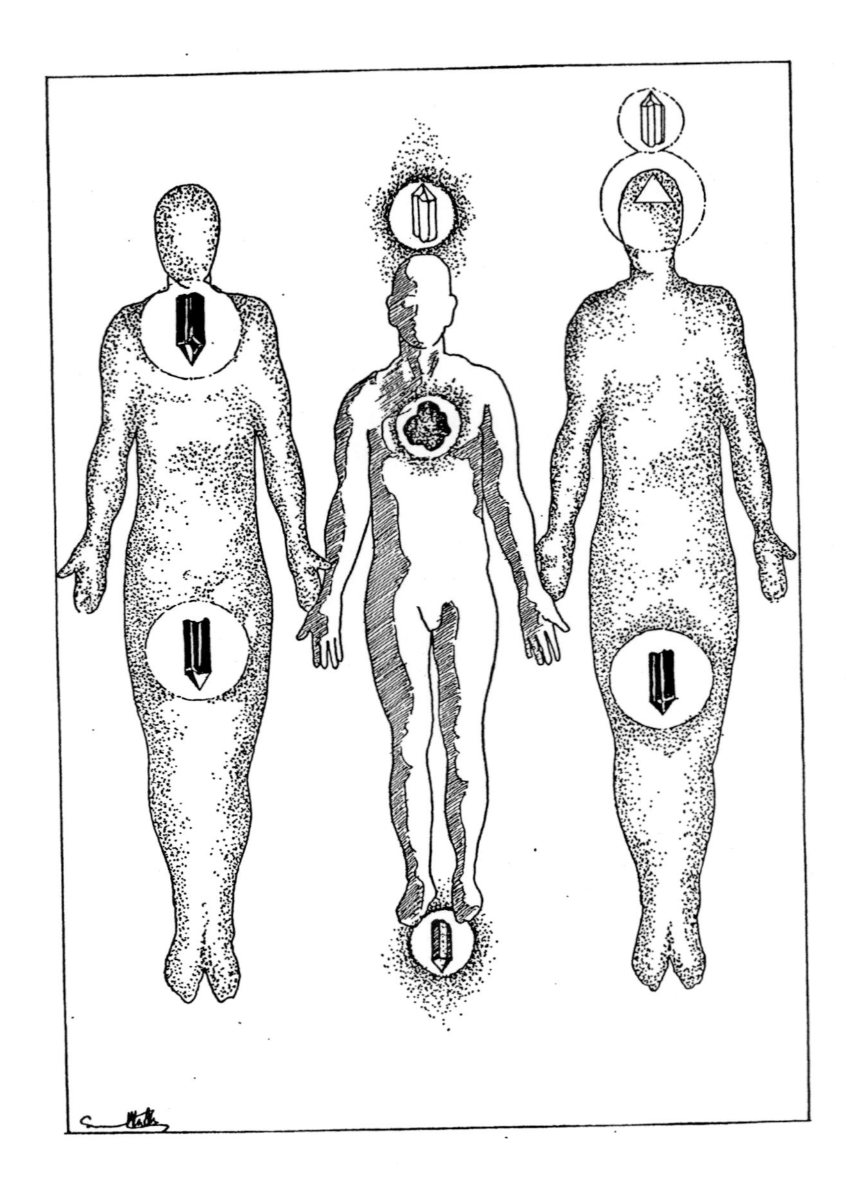

Introductory layouts: "Guidelines"

Guidelines for using nets

When using a crystal net it is important to follow some guidelines:-

1) Always allow yourself plenty of space and time - never squeeze a crystal net in between other appointments. It is always advisable to take several minutes to settle down and focus on how you feel before lying down in the net. This will allow the possibility of clearer experiences and the ability to notice changes more easily.

2) Different people will experience different sensations in the nets depending on their energy patterns. Experience will probably differ from one session to another, again depending on the individual's energies and those of the environment.

3 It is a good idea not to enter an energy net if you are very tired - you are more likely to fall asleep than experience anything. Unless, of course, your reason for entering a net is either to fall asleep or to wake yourself up!

4) At first it is often only by contrast that you will notice changes between how you feel in and out of the net. It is always better to spend a short time regularly in the net than spend a long time occasionally.

5) The maximum time we suggest you stay in any one net is twenty minutes. (Don't worry if you accidentally go over this time, however). We find that the experience deepens every four or five minutes. There is a definite shift of energy, a sinking to a new level. So the natural finishing times are five, ten, fifteen and twenty minutes or thereabouts. You will soon get used to the feel of the

end of one period and the beginning of another as there is a tendency to "float back up to the surface" before the next dive begins. It is less of a jar to the system to end a session as you are moving outwards towards ordinary consciousness than to break while on an inwards/ downward arc.

6) Always take time to come round to everyday activity slowly. Ideally you should have twice the time you have been in the net before you need to do anything focussed. This will give the body time to integrate the energies it has experienced into its normal everyday functioning.

Allow any feelings of impatience, fidgeting or restlessness to disappear BEFORE you resume normal activity.

7) Make sure that you will not be disturbed while you are in the net and during the rest period afterwards.

8) If at any time you feel discomfort or anxiety whilst in the net, quietly get up and find somewhere to relax until the sensations disappear. Re-enter the net or end the session and remain relaxing for a while.

9) There are several crystal layouts which can be used before or after using a crystal net. A few minutes, (between five and ten minutes) will be sufficient to rebalance energies.

9a) For initial balancing and calming:

Place a clear quartz point outwards at the crown of the head, rose quartz at the heart and smoky quartz, point downwards, close to the base of the spine.

9b) For disorientation or "feeling out of sorts" Clear quartz at crown of head, lapis lazuli or turquoise at the centre of the forehead and a smoky quartz between the legs close to the spine.

9c) For grounding, bringing down to earth, back to reality:

Smoky quartz at the throat, just above the collar bones, and smoky quartz at the base of spine, between the legs.

10) Unless specified otherwise all crystal nets should be laid out so that the head is aligned with magnetic north. This places the individual's bioelectromagnetic field in harmony with the flow of the earth's energy field.

11) Drinking a little pure water before and after each crystal net session can help both with the removal of toxicity often released and with the integration of new information and experience.

12) It is very important that all crystals used in these nets are cleansed before and after use. This ensures that any residual disharmonies are removed from the stone. There are many different ways to cleanse crystals:

a) hold the crystals under running water for a couple of minutes and allow to dry naturally

b) pass the crystals through incense smoke or smudge

c) place inside a resonant sound source - singing bowl, bell

d) wipe with pennyroyal or quartz essence

13) Keep a piece of paper and pen handy for when you finish. Make notes, drawings, scribbles, of your experiences as soon as you leave the net. Otherwise you

will forget the more subtle aspects of your experience. If you "hear" words or phrases these can often be the quickest to disappear or change.Write them down as you remember them - interpret later, at your leisure.

14) It can be interesting to begin by experiencing one net, followed by another, to notice the differences i.e. Moon followed by Mercury.

15) If you don't have a cloth of the preferred colour, then use a white cloth, or a white cloth with a colour filter, colour tincture or light essence.

16) Some "netters" experience a welter of visual imagery whilst others are focussed more on how they feel emotionally or sensations in the body. Neither is "better" than the other - different people translate the energy shifts in terms or language they are familiar with. Sometimes the kinesthetic (feeling) person gets a clearer idea what a net is about - visual imagery, like dream images, need some interpretation. It can take more sessions to identify a pattern in the types of image presented. Ideally a good balance of all the senses will give the fullest experience. So if you do favour one sense try to spend some time in a net focussing on the others. If you are visual, get used to feeling how the body is, what your mood is; if you are kinesthetic, watch your thoughts carefully.

Summary of uses for each net

Elemental nets

FIRE: Warming the physical body; improving circulation and digestion; enhancing all aspects of "fire"; contact with archetypal element of Fire.

Red Cloth - 2 rubies, 2 garnets, 2 topaz

EARTH: Aligning physical structure especially skeletal; clearing and protecting from negativity; aligning to Earth energies; harmonising with earth energies.

Green Cloth - 8 black tourmaline

AIR: Revitalising; removing confusion;aura cleansing; sense of personal space.

Yellow Cloth - 6 clear quartz crystals

WATER: Digestive system; subtle levels of communication; flow of creativity; flexibility; block removal.

Blue Cloth - 4 rose quartz, 1 clear quartz, 1 sapphire

ETHER: Celestial influences; spiritual uplifting and cleansing; removal from worldly problems; fine levels of inspiration.

White Cloth - 7 small clusters of celestite crystals

ELEMENTARY PARTICLES: Experiencing fine levels of creation, space and time.

Yellow Cloth - 6 or 8 celestite crystals, 1 piece of moldavite

Planetary nets

SUN: Energising; the Self; balance; improved circulation; contact with solar energies; clarity

Yellow Cloth - 6 rubies

MOON: Soothing; calming body and emotions; attunement and relief from lunar influences; digestive system; reproductive organs.

Dark Blue Cloth - 5 pieces of moonstone

MERCURY: energies of Mercury; communication; skills; adaptability; thought; clarity of mind; coordination.

Golden Yellow Cloth - 3 citrine, 3 clear quartz

VENUS: Creativity and artistic abilities; self-acceptance; relating to others; sexual tensions; energies of Venus.

Green Cloth - 3 rose quartz, 2 clear quartz

MARS: Motivation; Will; removing blocks to progress; energy boost; life-force; balance of aggression and motivation; libido; energies of Mars.

Red Cloth - 9 clusters of clear quartz

JUPITER: Laws of nature; expansion on every level; new concepts and images; positivity; growth; opportunities.

Blue Cloth - 12 clear quartz

SATURN: Patience and self-discipline; foundations; understanding; Time; removal of blocks to progress; practicality.

Pink Cloth - 4 clear quartz, 4 rose quartz

URANUS: Rebels; non-conformists; group awareness; intuition; invention; electromagnetic stress; illumination.

Pink Cloth - 6 clear quartz, six green stones

NEPTUNE: Inspiration; psychic perceptions; creative imagination; focus; fine aspects of creation; boundaries; addictions.

Blue Cloth - 5 smoky quartz, 16 pieces of natural chalk

PLUTO: Hidden things; the unconscious; renewal of life-force; understanding processes of life and death; cleansing; purification; inhibitions.

Black or Red Cloth - 5 pieces of dark obsidian

CHIRON: Core beliefs; fundamental blocks to progress, hidden skills; release from past hurt; courage; re-evaluation; insight.

Yellow Cloth - 6 pieces of turquoise

The Self

ACTIVATING PERSONAL POTENTIAL: Clearing emotional blocks; cleansing and healing; activates diverted skills; self-development; integration.

Yellow Cloth - 5 rose quartz, 5 clear quartz

CLARIFICATION ON ALL LEVELS: Understanding of any situation; removal of obstacles to understanding; clarity

Green Cloth - 5 clear quartz, 2 rubies or topaz, 1 piece of moldavite, 1 black tourmaline

WHOLE ENTITY ENERGIES: Awareness of multi-dimensional Self; information of all sorts; alignment to Higher Self; true direction; self-integration; confidence

White Cloth - 5 pieces of moldavite, 4 amethyst, 3 clear quartz

FINE LEVEL I: Addition to other nets to deepen experience; speeds healing; detoxification; link to personal source.

Orange Cloth - 3 smoky quartz

FINE LEVEL II: Integration of subtle bodies; planetary transits; different levels of consciousness and reality.

Dark Pink Cloth - 1 black tourmaline, 2 green tourmaline, 1 blue tourmaline, 1 pink tourmaline

AMETHYST HEALING: Deep healing work, safe regressions, clarity of perceptions, calming mind.

Yellow or Violet Cloth - 8 amethyst (points preferred)

Colour Keys

RED - THE CHRIST: Energy to achieve; being oneself; empowerment; protection; relinquishing guilt; reality.

White Cloth - 12 clear quartz, 1 ruby

ORANGE - LAO TSU: Healing and compassion; deep cleansing and purifying; detoxification; wisdom and humour; creativity.

Orange Cloth - 12 smoky quartz

GOLD - SANAT KUMARA: Creative organising skills; loving intelligence; solar system; wisdom from Higher Self; mental functioning.

Yellow Cloth - 12 clear quartz, 1 citrine

YELLOW - LADY PORTIA: Mental clarity; discernment; balance at all levels; truth; destiny.
Blue Cloth - 7 lapis lazuli pieces, 5 clear quartz (tumbled)

PALE YELLOW - KUTHUMI: Releasing fears and anxieties; joy; expansion; harmony; bliss; free flow of information; attunement to animal kingdoms.

Yellow Cloth - 6 clear quartz

PALE GREEN - HILARION: Personal space; freedom; true direction and Path; clarification of spiritual direction; attunement to Earth and its life - especially plant kingdoms; calmness.

Black Cloth - 7 pieces of moldavite, 1 green tourmaline, 5 tourmaline of other colours.

DARK GREEN - DJWHAL KHUL: Rediscovering and re-applying forgotten knowledge; distant parts of the galaxies; stars etc.; astrological clarity; innovation; outsiders; heretics; aliens.

Black Cloth - 12 pieces of moldavite

TURQUOISE - MAHA CHOHAN: Personal expression of soul; individuality; innovation; maintaining and strengthening immune system.

Green Cloth - 3 celestite, 3 moldavite

BLUE - EL MORYA: serenity; peacefulness; creative potential; communication and expression; aligning Self to Higher Will.

Blue Cloth - 6 celestite, 6 coloured tourmaline

VIOLET - ST GERMAIN: Activating healing energy; personal potential; imagination and inspiration; integration of Spirit with Matter; understanding ritual and ceremony.

Yellow Cloth - 8 amethyst

WHITE - SERAPIS BEY: Purification; cleansing; protection; renewal and rebirth.

White or Black Cloth - 6 clear quartz, 6 black tourmaline

PINK - NADA: All issues of self-worth; universal love and compassion; tolerance; forgiveness; nurturing; creativity; fine levels of consciousness; subtle aspects of sound and vibration; all aggressive states.

Mid-pink or Dark Pink cloth - 12 rose quartz

MAGENTA PINK - PALLAS ATHENE: Protected space; equilibrium; calming fears; assertiveness; balancing polarities.

Deep Pink Cloth - 8 clear quartz

PALE BLUE/PINK - ORION AND ANGELICA: Connection to Earth consciousness; endings and beginning; protective and supporting; galactic awareness; understanding the cycles of time.

Pale Pink Cloth - 3 rose quartz, 3 celestite, 3 smoky quartz

Chakra templates

BASE: Survival; energy; grounding; centreing; motivation; practicality.

4 clear quartz, 4 dark tourmaline, 1 red, black or brown stone.

SACRAL: Sexual problems; stabilising emotions; sensuality; detoxification; anger; frustration; creativity; pleasure.

3 clear quartz, rutilated quartz or herkimer diamond
3 moonstone, rose quartz, lapis lazuli or amethyst

SOLAR PLEXUS: Personal power and ability; joy, laughter, spontaneity; confidence; immune system; digestive and nervous system; relaxation.

3 citrine, 3 garnets, 1 of either ruby, tiger's eye, jasper, garnet or pyrites.

HEART: Integration; balance; freedom; calm; discrimination; knowing your own desires and needs; self-worth; love.

1 rose quartz, 4 green tourmaline, 4 smoky quartz
1 clear quartz/pink stone, 1 herkimer diamond (optional)

THROAT: Self expression; communication skills; enlivening mind; understanding

1 blue stone, 1 turquoise or chrysocolla, 2 double-terminated crystals, 1 clear quartz

BROW: Seeing and understanding; increased perception; imagination; intuition; visualisation; enthusiasm.

1 lapis lazuli or herkimer diamond, 3 fluorites, 1 blue or violet fluorite

CROWN: Fulfilment; understanding; bliss; increased energy and vitality; links to universal energy.

3 clear quartz, plus optional stones

The elements

Introduction to the elemental nets

The Elements these nets encompass have nothing to do with current scientific terminology. The division of physical existence or matter into discreet parts: Earth, Water, Air and Fire, is as old as the concepts of time and place, as old as the awareness of being "here and now".

The Elements are a fundamental conceptualisation of the qualities of existence. They are the building blocks for most of humanity's cosmologies. The number of Elements may change from culture to culture but the significance is constant.

In a way each Element is the lowest common denominator, the largest sub-set of one aspect of human perception. From a current scientific point of view the Elements are simplistic, primitive notions of what goes to make up matter. From the level of practical human existence and from the level of understanding of wholes ("gestalts" - the big pictures), the Elements describe everything perfectly and satisfactorily. The concept of the Elements is psychologically useful and "right".

They are, as it were, the archetypes of matter. Like their companions, the archetypes of human mental patterns, it is possible to dismiss them as wishful thinking or fantasy, but that won't make any difference to their raw power and presence. Those who have, magically or otherwise, contacted some small expression of an Elemental power will know just how mindbogglingly unrestrained, powerful and dangerously seductive such a contact can be to the balance of the human mind.

Whether they are a purely human construct or some truly "objective" phenomena, the Elements have travelled down through history with us. Fire, Earth, Air and Water are as much a part of us as North, South, East and West or Spring, Summer, Autumn and Winter. They are a way of mapping who, what and where we are in the "here and now". They are one of the compasses to let us explore existence without getting totally lost and confused.

The qualities of each Element and the way in which the Elements interact builds a satisfying and magical reason for the way things are. In order to be balanced in body and mind the Elements within us must also be balanced. Many, if not all, traditional healing systems assess the degree of imbalance of the Elements and aim to correct any over-proponderance of one Element with the addition of its opposite. For example, a fiery, hot inflammation will be treated with cooling, watery herbs whilst something like an oedema that shows an excess of cold, watery conditions may be treated with a remedy that increases the Elements of Fire and Air.

The Ayurvedic healing system of India, the Chinese Five Elements, the Classical Greek and Roman system of Humours that the Arabs taught to medieval Europe, the healing systems of the American tribes utilising the Medicine Wheel all rely on the Elements for their effectiveness.

We can use the Elemental nets in this rebalancing way to help regain our own bearings. Firstly, though, we need to have clear experience of each Element in its pure state - to experience Fire, Earth, Air, Water and Ether within our own natures. Once we have these benchmarks we might be able to see which elements predominate, which are over-enthusiastic and which we are studiously ignoring because we are quite happy being a shopping trolley with a sticky wheel (going round in small circles).

Fire net

What you need

A red cloth. Six crystals in all: two of ruby, two garnets and two topaz. Different combinations of these stones can be used, but this is perhaps the most balanced. We have found that there is a slightly different effect when the stones are placed in each other's places. For an overall effect topaz is placed at the top of the head and below the feet; ruby is placed by the right shoulder, garnet by the left shoulder; ruby is placed to the outside of the left hand, garnet to the outside of the right hand.

What this net can be used for

Warming the physical body; aiding and improving circulation and digestion;enhancing all levels of "fire"; contact with the archetypal element.

If, instead of ruby and garnet being placed diagonally opposite, the same stone is on either side of the body you will notice there will be an increased warming of the feet and legs, particularly if garnet is placed at the head and feet, rubies by the hands and topaz by the shoulders.

Rubies are associated with the heart chakra, the physical heart and circulation as well as the base chakra at the bottom of the spine. As such it has a natural tendency to increase the vitality and energy within the body.

Garnet,and we are speaking here of the rich red variety, is perhaps one of the most effective stones for giving a kick of energy unadulterated by any other vibration. Garnet is unusual in that when it is cut into a faceted stone it often becomes even more powerful. Garnet naturally aligns itself to the raw, driving, survival energy of the base chakra - the roll-

Fire net

up-your-sleeves-and-get-down-to-it enjoyment of simply doing and acting in the world. This energy acts as a remedy to those with cold feet, both physically and metaphorically, for there is a subtle link between poor circulation in the extremities of the body and an unwillingness somewhere within the individual's thought patterns to fully partake of the act of living for fear of losing out. That many more women suffer from poor circulation in their limbs than men may be linked to cultural pressure, where women are expected to be less assertive, less demonstrative and less creative than males, and also more prone to body-image problems.

The lines of crystallisation which appear on a natural topaz are a clue to its function. Whenever a crystal shows parallel striations along its length it is certain to be able to deal with energy transformations, increasing the flow of energy and unblocking stagnant or negative areas. Topaz relaxes tension in the body and activates the solar plexus chakra which is the centre that integrates all incoming energies for the body's benefit. So while ruby and garnet energise and motivate, topaz ensures the energy is evenly transmitted throughout the system.

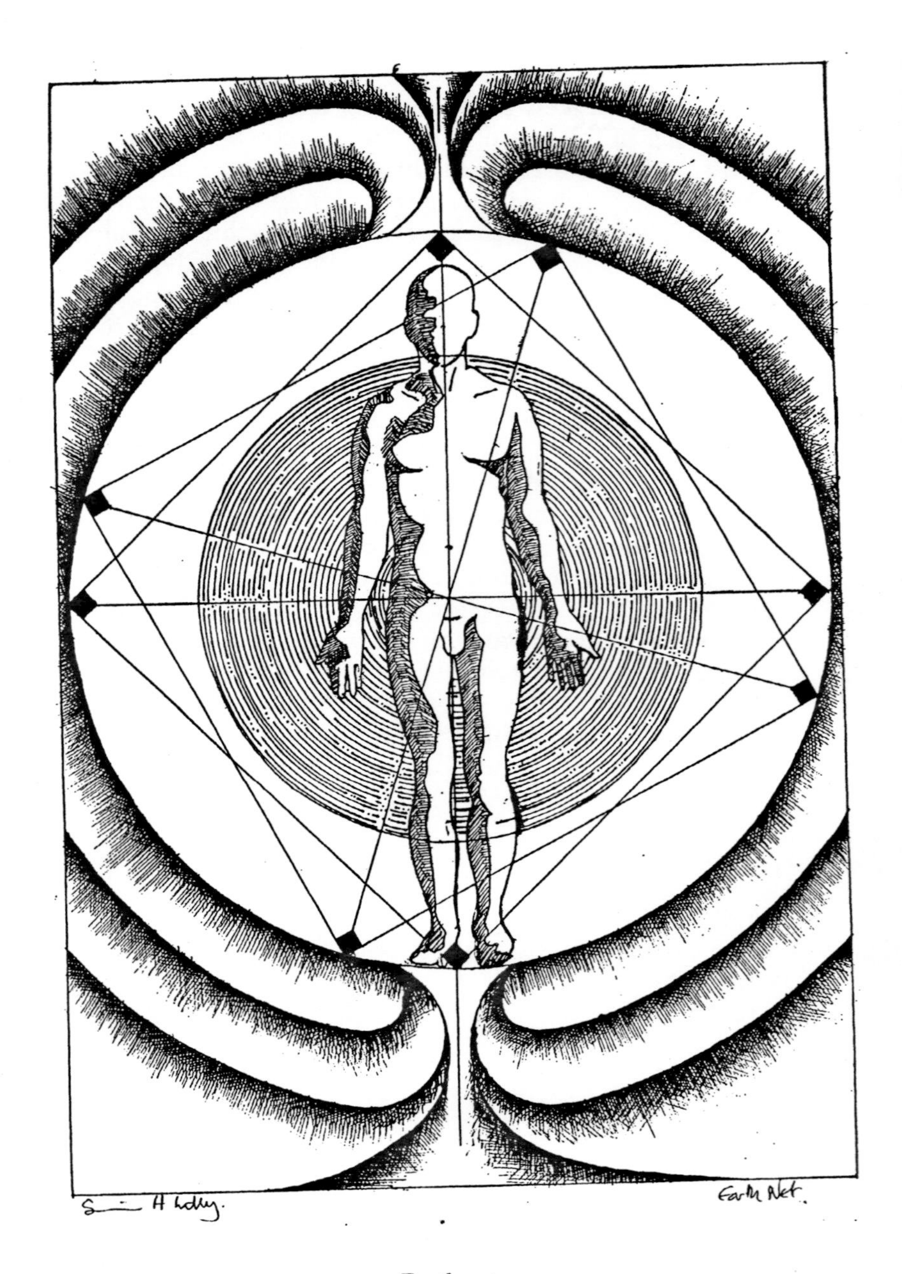

Earth net

Earth net

What you need

Eight black tourmaline crystals, a green cloth.

If your tourmaline crystals have natural terminations these should be placed inwards towards the body. The crystals are to make two intersecting squares. The first square will be made of four tourmalines, one at the head, one at the feet, one either side of the body. If you are lying with your head to the north this square is now aligned to the cardinal directions. The second square is made with the remaining four crystals about 20 to 25 degrees clockwise to the first. All crystals point inwards to the body.

What this net can be used for

Aligning and balancing the physical structure, bones, muscles etc.; clearing and protecting from negative environmental influences; aligning to the earth's energies; harmonising with the specific place you are in.

If you have some aches and pains this net may initially emphasise the discomfort, but you will find it soon passes. Very often there is a sensation of great weight, or sometimes of lightness. It is regularly reported that there is a feeling of subtle manipulation and rearrangement of overtense or misaligned structures.

Tourmaline is an unusual and very useful mineral. It is found in nearly every colour, though the black variety, schorl, is the commonest in Europe.

Unlike many other minerals, the colour is not the result of minute amounts of impurities, but is caused by a change of the chemical structure itself. When it is gently heated one end of a crystal will become positively charged whilst the other end becomes negative.

Tourmaline is traditionally one of those stones which protects the wearer from negativity. A stone of the appropriate colour activates the corresponding chakra. In this net the use of schorl links to the base chakra, which acts as our connection to the earth and is a grounding device for excess energies. This provides the stability and sense of security upon which the other chakra centres build.

In the Earth Net we reconnect with the planet itself. This can be very useful after we have moved house or done a lot of long-distance travelling. Tourmaline may well help to reduce the symptoms of jetlag.

Tourmaline and the Earth Net have been used to good effect in dealing with tinnitus, whiplash, back and neck-ache and the disorientation caused by cranial plate and vertebral fixation.

The Earth Net can be used to attune to the essence of the planet Gaia herself, and also to attune to the element of earth, the fourth and densest of the classical elements, ruled by the elementals known as gnomes. For those wishing to link to the earth it may be useful to know that the note and key of F# has a natural resonance to the planet at a vibrational level.

Air net

What you need

Six clear quartz crystals, a yellow coloured cloth. The six quartz crystals, if naturally terminated, are all placed with points outwards. One is placed above the head, below the feet, at mid-thigh level by the hands and near each shoulder.

What this net can be used for

Blowing away cobwebs; helps to remove fatigue, mental cloudiness or confusion; cleanses the aura; brings back the feeling of personal space.

This net is very similar in pattern to the two intersecting triangles forming a six-pointed star, the Star of David or Seal of Solomon, which is often used by crystal workers to begin the process of clearing imbalances from the energy bodies. Here, with the addition of the vibration of yellow, given by the cloth, it is modified slightly to be more attuned to the level of mind which is associated with the element of Air.

The colour yellow has the energy necessary to stimulate the analytical, rational and discriminative faculties of the mind. It is one of the best colours to have around when one is studying as it keeps the mind sharp and aids the memory. It also wards off fatigue. The essential oil of lemon has the same qualities - just take a deep sniff and those cobwebs of fatigue melt away.

We often use the Air Net after a hard day's mental work or when the mind just can't shake off cloudy vagueness. Whereas the Mercury Net is stimulating and busy, the Air Net is like a cool breeze, light and refreshing.

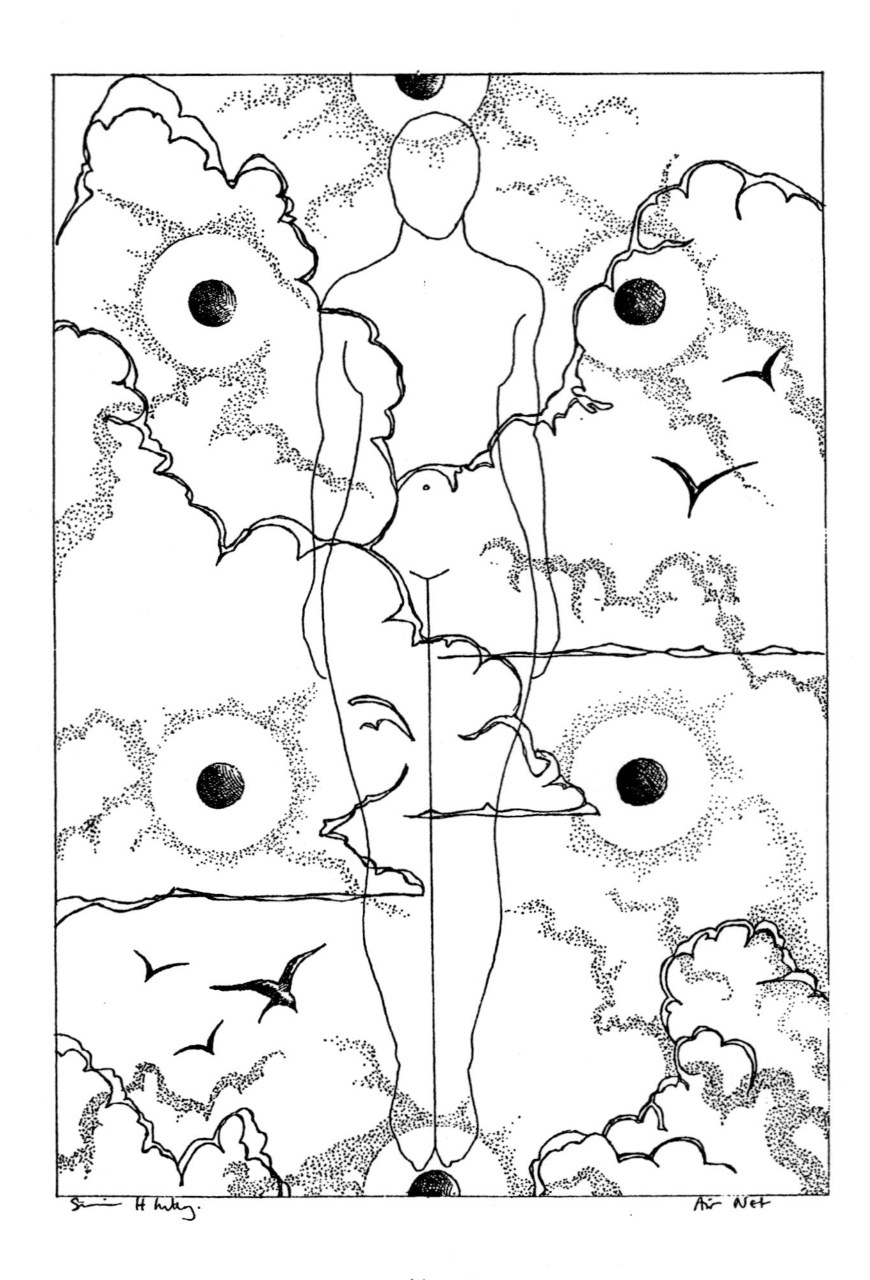

Air net

Water net

What you need

Four rose quartz, one clear quartz, a blue sapphire, and a blue cloth. The rose quartz are placed beside the feet and either side of the shoulders; the clear quartz is put at the thymus gland where the collar bones meet at the base of the throat; the sapphire rests above the top of the head.

What this net can be used for

Activating the digestive system; stimulating subtle levels of communication; the flow of creativity; flexibility; releasing blocks at many different levels.

Attuning to the element of water is attuning to the upholder of life. This simple compound of hydrogen and oxygen is the foundation of most life processes on this planet. Because it is so pervasive and its forms are so various the possible experiences within the energy net are manyfold and after a few try-outs it may be useful to set a finer focus on whatever aspect you wish to experience.

For example, there are the external manifestations of rivers, oceans, storm, and there are the internal experiences of bloodflow, digestive processes, the protoplasm of the cell. There are the symbolic qualities of passivity, flow, transformation, patience, equilibrium, release. There is the archetypal experience of water itself, the natural form of which is a sphere, and whose natural motion is the spiral expansion and contraction.

Due to the force of gravity on Earth these forms and tendencies become disguised, but they are ever-present and

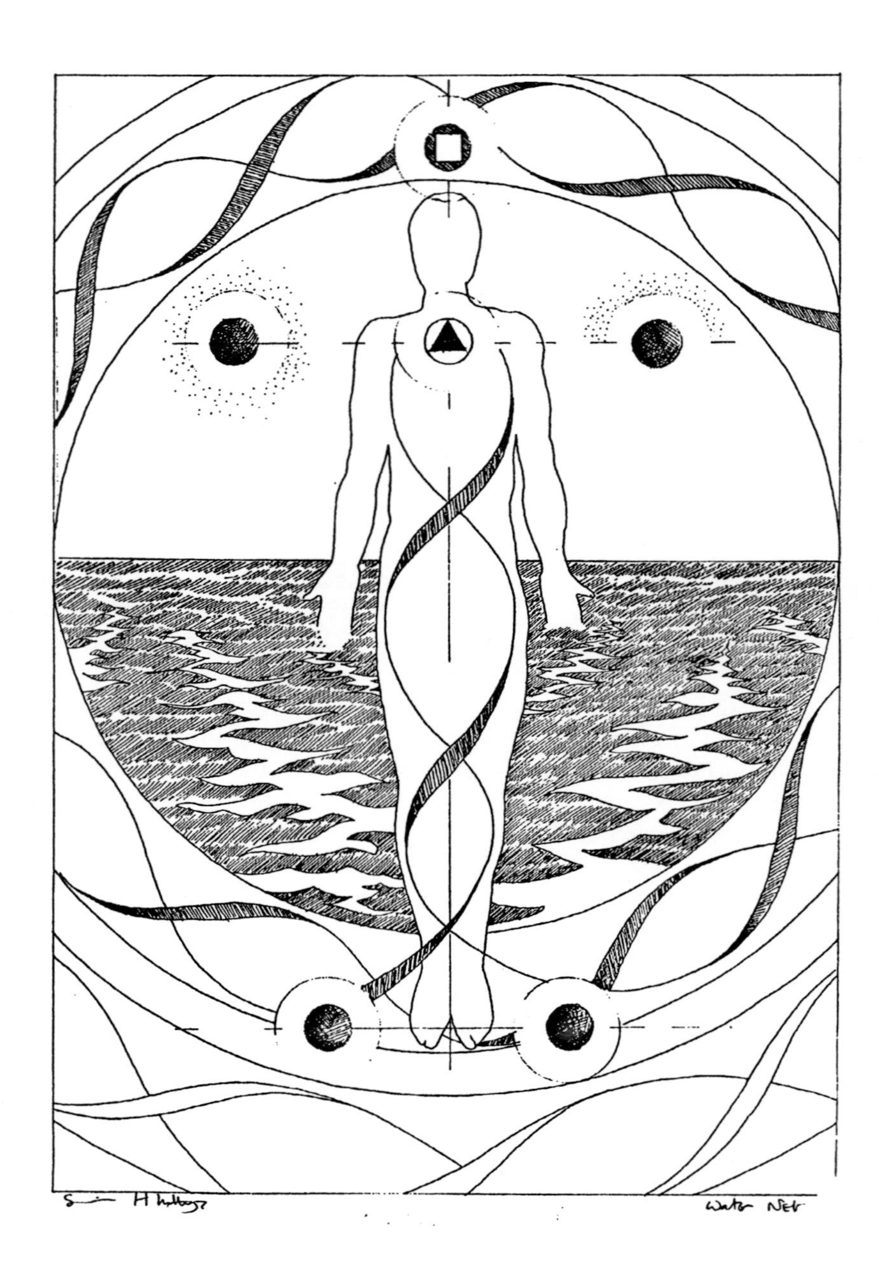

Water net

have shaped very precisely the form of creatures and their organs. Water becomes the vehicle and the vessel of expression for life: the container and also that which is contained.

Water is linked with the emotions. Both have the tendency to move, to flow outwards in order to attain a stillness or a point of equilibrium. When this flow is blocked in some way pressure continues to build up and unless released, can cause devastation when it finally breaks through. Someone who feels on the point of bursting, full of desperation, with energy circling in on itself (which might manifest in the body as overactive or out-of-control conditions), may find this net a way of gently releasing the internal pressure and restoring a new harmony.

Those who feel out of touch ("out of the flow", "stranded"), either emotionally or mentally, should also try this net.

The rose quartz helps to free these blocks in the energy systems of the body, particularly resolving emotional conflict. The clear quartz at the thymus gland strengthens the body's natural electromagnetic field and will have a beneficial effect on the immune and endocrine systems. Sapphire also works with the endocrine system and the digestive system. On a fine level sapphire helps to balance subtle energy systems which eases depressive emotional states and enhances the link between body, mind and spirit. This encourages the flow of information and energy. The blue cloth stimulates the throat chakra which functions through personal expression, communication, mental clarity and an increased sense of peace and peacefulness.

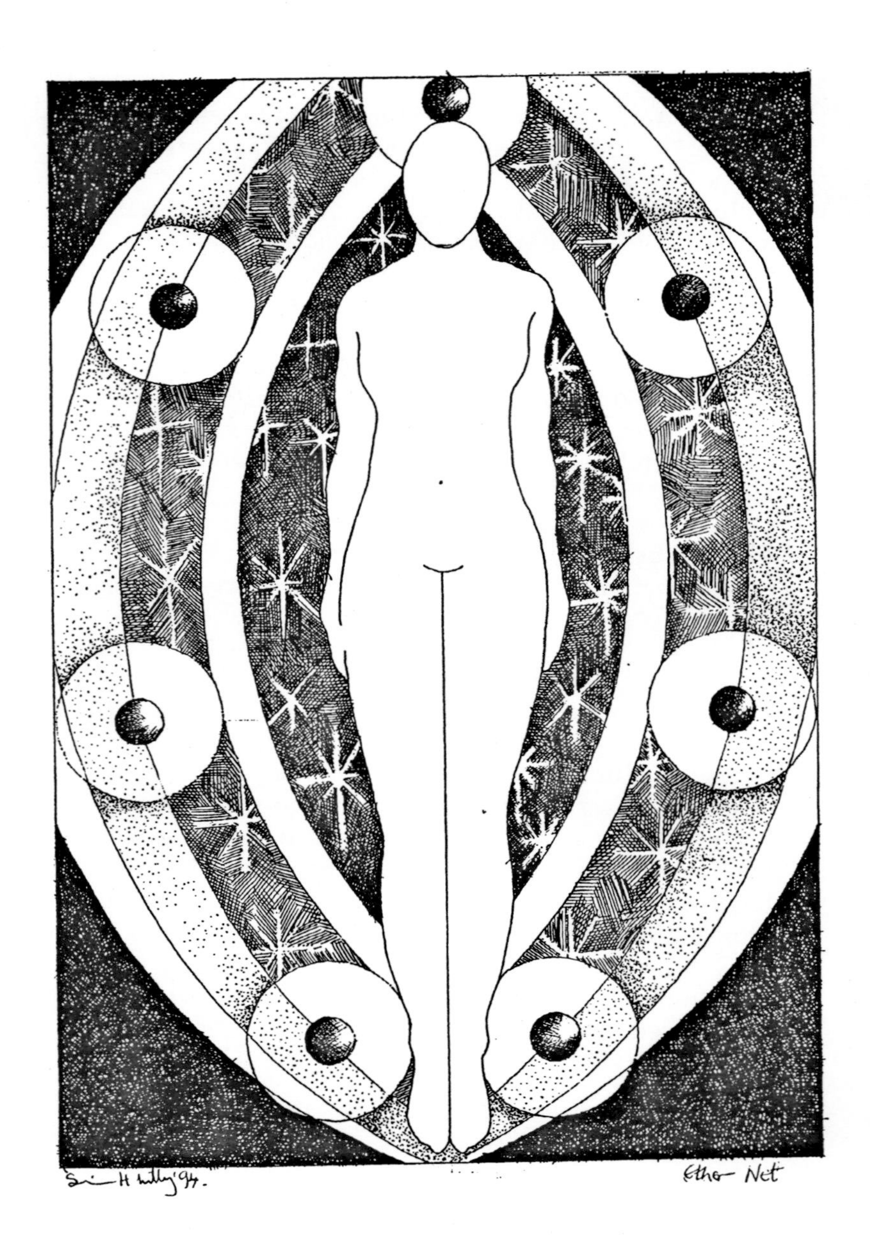

Ether net

Ether net

What you need

Seven small clusters of celestite. A white cloth. The seven clusters are placed above the head; upper arm level on both sides; to the outside of each hand; to the outside and level with each foot. (ie. evenly spaced around the body). If possible the clusters are placed with the points inwards towards the body.

What this net can be used for

Attuning to celestial influences; spiritual upliftment and cleansing; removal from worldly matters; fine levels of inspiration.

The fifth element, ether, is like a vessel that holds all the other elements of earth, air, fire and water. It is the medium through which these more dense elements manifest. Ether, (Sanskrit: "*akasha*"), is the ultimate substance, often defined as space itself. Because it is the finest of substances ether is potentially the most powerful. Tuning in to this level of creation can allow fine impulses of manifestation to appear in your life, either as new opportunities or as ideas and inspiration. Ether contains all possibilities of existence and so it is also that area where desires begin to become reality. The safeguard (or drawback!), to this is that, at fine levels of energy, only those impulses which align with the laws of the universe can survive. So don't use this net as a wishing well - it won't!

Akasha, or ether, also stores within itself impressions of all the interplay of the other elements, like a memory of everything that has ever happened. These are the so-called Akashic Records. Having attuned to the Ether Net it should be possible to "read" these records, which often appear as visions of what to "read" these records, which often appear as visions of what has long gone.

Celestite is a beautiful, pale blue mineral, usually from Madagascar, though it does exist in less spectacular forms elsewhere (ie. Yate, Gloucestershire). Many people who just pick up a piece for the first time are aware of a increase in joyfulness and bliss, a sudden lifting of mood and clarity of perceptions. The delicate colour and the clear blue crystals often look as they are at the boundary of this world and some other more angelic realm. In fact, celestite helps one to attune to more spiritual states and to usefully communicate and integrate information thus gained. Its blue colour naturally aligns it to the throat chakra, so celestite is beneficial in all creative and artistic endeavours, and brings a sense of calm and clarity to all matters.

Celestite is sometimes quite difficult and expensive to obtain, and although clusters are usually easier to find than single crystals, it may take some hunting to find small affordable clusters for this net.

Several nets require clusters rather than points. The group effect of a cluster gives a more powerful but more non-directional and diffusive energy, a scattering effect as if each cluster were a showerhead spraying the area around it with its energy vibration.

The white cloth used here gives a clear, clean background energy from which anything can be drawn forth, (much like the colours of the rainbow split from white light). White is the colour of unlimited potential and purity and so is in harmony with the celestial energies of celestite.

We have found this net to be one of the most popular at workshops, indeed, it sometimes requires considerable persuasion to move on to the next one! As the energies involved are very fine, be extra careful that you do not spend overlong in the Ether Net, and make sure you have plenty of time to come back down to earth afterwards!

A peculiar characteristic of this and some other fine level nets is that, whilst the person in the net feels quite warm and comfortable, those tuning in from the outside notice a distinct change in temperature as if a cool, mountain breeze were blowing from somewhere. With some other nets the experience is of a heating effect.

Elementary particles

Attunement to elementary particles net

What you need

Eight celestite crystals and one moldavite, or six celestite and one moldavite. (There are two variations to this net which can either be used separately or together). A yellow cloth.

In the first arrangement the moldavite is placed between the knees. Five celestite crystals, points inwards, are placed in an arc around the legs and feet making sure they extend no higher than the moldavite. One celestite is placed above the crown of the head. The second arrangement moves the moldavite up to the solar plexus and an arc of seven celestites surrounds the body from this point downwards. The celestite above the head is moved slightly further away from the body.

What this net can be used for

Experiencing finer levels of creation, space and time.

This net is really for research and investigation. Experience has taught that it can prove somewhat disorienting and confusing at first. It is sometimes easier to experience the first variation for a few minutes and then change to the second pattern to deepen and integrate the energies. As we tune into finer levels of creation we experience the universe through vibration, pattern and interaction of forces. It can stretch the perceptions and mental structures because the experiences fall outside of what we usually regard as "real life". However, if we are becoming aware of deep levels of energy, the building blocks of life in fact, regular use of this net should allow us to extend our senses beyond the normal, making us more aware of the interplay of forces in our lives, of the patterns that make up our existence, and freeing us from the rigid concepts of time and space so that we can make the most out of our surroundings.

The nature of what elementary particles are and how they are seen will depend on one's frame of reference. Nowadays we tend to think in semi-scientific terms of very small sub-atomic particles - the constituents of smaller and smaller bits of atoms whizzing around huge accelerators and showing up for a brief moment as a trail of light spinning through a bubble chamber before disappearing. The fact that these bits of existence have some peculiar habits, like moving backwards and forwards in time and effecting each other at great distances, ensures they hover somewhere between the mysterious and the mystical. In another cultural framework experience of these objects might be equated with spirits and gods rather than electromagnetic forces.

How we define our experience depends upon how we have been taught to label things, upon how we use our senses of perception and how we experience time. Time is dependent on our metabolic rate. We see the world as we do because of the speed of our nerve impulses and the amount of information that can be received and processed at any moment. For instance, consider the metabolic rate of a tree. One inhalation is one of our days, an outbreath is one of our nights, (plants absorb CO_2 during daylight and release O_2 at night). So as far as a tree is concerned twenty-four hours is one breath cycle.

In such a way of measurement a human year might be just a day and night to the tree, where spring and summer are the active "day" and autumn and winter the quieter, introspective "night". Now imagine how a tree would perceive the human and animal life going on around it. If they were noticed at all it would probably be as small and very rapid changes of pressure, or a slight vibration which would appear and disappear as if from nowhere. In fact, very similar perceptions to a scientist looking at the behaviour of sub-atomic particles!

If this imagination is extended to cover the life-cycle and metabolic rate, and therefore the perceptive ability of a crystal, a star, a universe, a bacterium, an atom and so on, you will begin to see that the nature of reality and the interaction of energies may be constant, yet the perception of what is real has infinite variability.

Celestite brings the strong sense of harmony and joy characteristic of the finer levels of creation, as well as the ability to process the delicate subtleties of information. Moldavite, a bottle-green translucent stone found in a small area of Czechoslovakia, is probably the result of a meteor impact over fourteen million years ago. It is a wonderful stone for amplifying and deepening experience, particularly subtle perceptions and healing ability, and it increases the connection to more universal, off-planet energies. Moldavite is a finite resource and so tends to be fairly expensive, but it is well worth looking out for small pieces to buy.

The yellow cloth will help the mind to stay alert and to analyse and organise its perceptions. Yellow helps to define boundaries and discreet forms, and helps to maintain self-awareness essential when dealing with such a boggling subject.

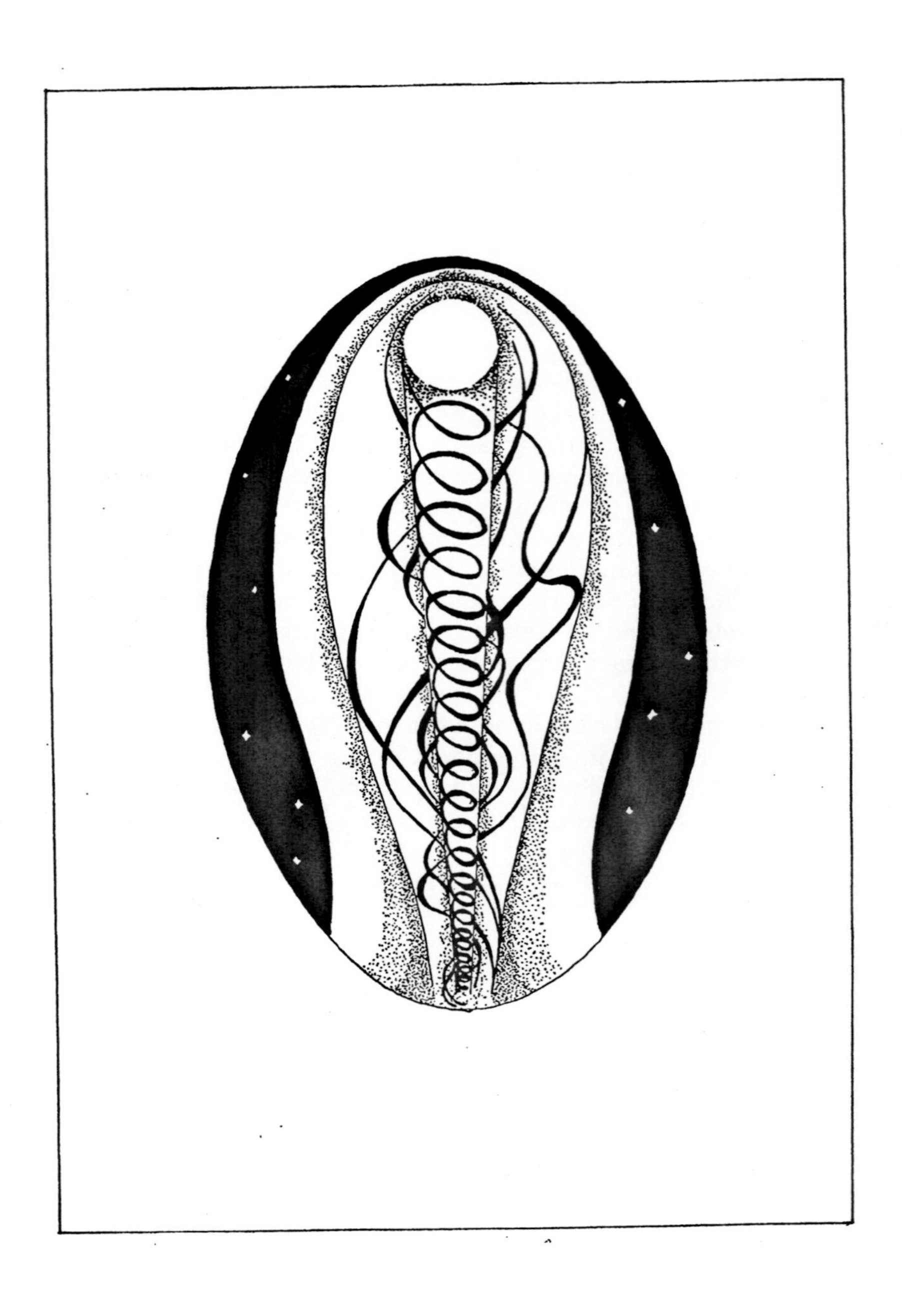

Planetary nets

Introduction to planetary nets

We are used to thinking of the planets as being "out there" far off in the solar system, sometimes visible in our night skies, sometimes of temporary interest if one of them is the focus of unusual events. There is a grudging acceptance that planetary gravitational fields can produce terrestrial events such as increased tectonic activity, but apart from astrologers, few people consider the planets at all relevant to everyday life. This was not the case in the past.

Not only were the intellectuals aware of the tides of planetary influences, but craftspeople, healers, herbalists, gardeners, farmers, as well as apothecaries, astrologers and magicians, took it for granted that it was essential to know the times of planetary ascendance. Not only were days under the influence of a particular planet and were so named (Sun day, Moon day etc.) but each day and night were also divided into planetary "hours", where time between sunrise and sunset was equally divided amongst the planets beginning with the ruler of that day. Depending on the nature of activity the appropriate planetary hour was chosen for the task. A plant under the rulership of Mars was to be collected during the rulership of that planet so that it would be at its most potent. A medicine was prepared and then taken at a particular time. Nowadays all this may seem to be nothing more than superstition but it served as a means to integrate human activity with the larger, macrocosmic movements of the planets - it helped our forebears to belong within Creation in a way few of us today can hope to experience.

We know more about the nature of the local space we move through than at any other time in history and yet we feel no greater understanding, or sense of belonging - if anything a cool, scientific objectivity has driven away much of the significance of human existence. A satisfying, workable cosmology - the essential foundation for any psychologically stable and healthy society - is simply lacking. Rich mythological reality is replaced by a sterile, clinical fact-gathering.

Let us look at the solar system as an entity in its own right. With the sun at its centre and the planets revolving in their specific orbits it is commonly thought that Pluto marks the outermost limit of the system. The outer "skin" of the Sun's body is however another four million miles beyond the orbit of Pluto in what is called the Oort clouds. Here, at the outermost edge of the Sun's gravitational field revolves a barrier of dust, gas and rock, which when perturbed by more distant cosmic events can send comets spinning towards the inner planets.

The Sun and its planetary bodies, comets and Oort clouds is not stationary in space like a volvox floating in a pool. It flies at over 48,000 miles an hour on an outer arm of the Milky Way, which itself turns around a huge cluster of other galaxies at 1,350,000 miles per hour. This viewed through a time span of about a hundred years, our solar system resembles a comet, the Sun at the head with planets spinning out orbital spirals behind it at different rates. The planetary organs are bathed in the solar wind and each body interacts to create complex electromagnetic circuits and gravitational tides.

With this view of our solar system, as if seen by a being with a metabolic rate perhaps a hundred times slower than our own, the solar system swims a long spiral 30,000 million miles long heading through space between the constellations of Lyra and Hercules*. With such a view, the universe ceases to resemble a neat clockwork mechanism and appears more like an evanescent play of sunlight on the rippling surface of water.

* From L Blair " *Rhythms of Vision*" and R Collin "*The Theory of Celestial Influence*"

Sun net

What you need

Six rubies and a yellow cloth. The rubies are equally spaced around the body, one at the top of the head, one below the feet, two near the knees, two near the elbows.

What this net can be used for

Energising, tuning back into the Self, balance, improved circulation, contact with solar energies, clarity.

The most usual experience in this net is a gentle warming, a bringing together and focusing of one's attention on the self. The rubies to be used don't have to be of gem quality! It is quite easy to acquire small ruby crystals for a couple of pounds each and these will be perfectly sufficient.

Ruby is the red variety of the hard mineral, corundum. In Vedic astrology ruby is the stone of the sun, and as the sun is the central point of the solar system so is ruby the stone whose primary influence is on the heart chakra, the central balancing point of the human energy system. Any dysfunction or weakness of the heart or circulation can be helped with ruby. Problems with the physical heart are often related to excessive responsibility for others, which is one aspect of an unbalanced heart chakra. Ruby can help with these issues, particularly where an active leadership role is being played, ie. managers and business people.

Problems with the circulatory system can be triggered by an imbalance in this flow of heart energy, which could be called love, either throughout the individual, or aspects of the individual, or between the self and others. Not loving the

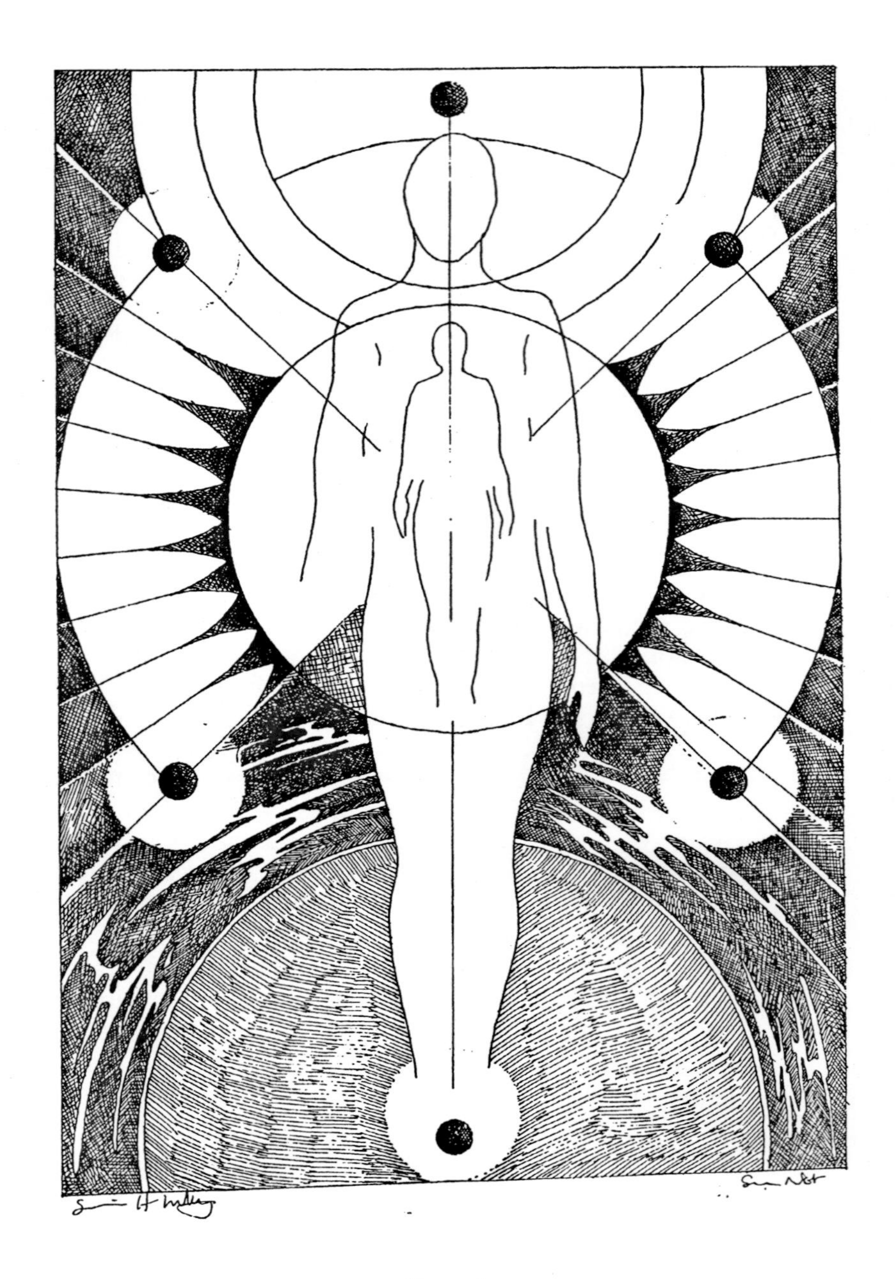

Sun net

whole self equally is like preventing the sun from shining on some parts of a garden - eventually what lives there will start to suffer and finally perish. As the sun is the essential constituent of physical life, so love (energy from the heart and heart chakra), is the essential nutrient that the self needs to grow and develop. Individuals with cold hands or cold feet may sometimes be showing that there is some part of themselves holding back from a full participation in the world. This is where "cold feet" equates with fear of action. Often this is caused by a lack of confidence, a lack of security, a fear of letting go on some level or other. The Sun Net will gently warm those dark corners, bringing a deep relaxation and allowing the heart energy to feed all parts of the self equally. The Sun Net may also be of help to those of us who feel desperately low during the winter months when there is little sunshine to warm and cheer us.

The sun is the symbolic presence of the Highest Self within us - the central source of life and energy. The mantra that allows us to attune to this Self and to the centre of our living solar system is AUM HRIM HAMSA SURYAYE NAMAH AUM.

The famous Gayatri mantra is the hymn to the sun sung at sunrise. It can be interpreted on many different levels and is the verbal equivalent of the energy by which our sun manifested itself and its planetary centres: AUM TAT SAVITUR VARENYAM BHARGO DEVASYA DHIMAHI DHIYO YO NAH PRACHADAYAT. AUM.

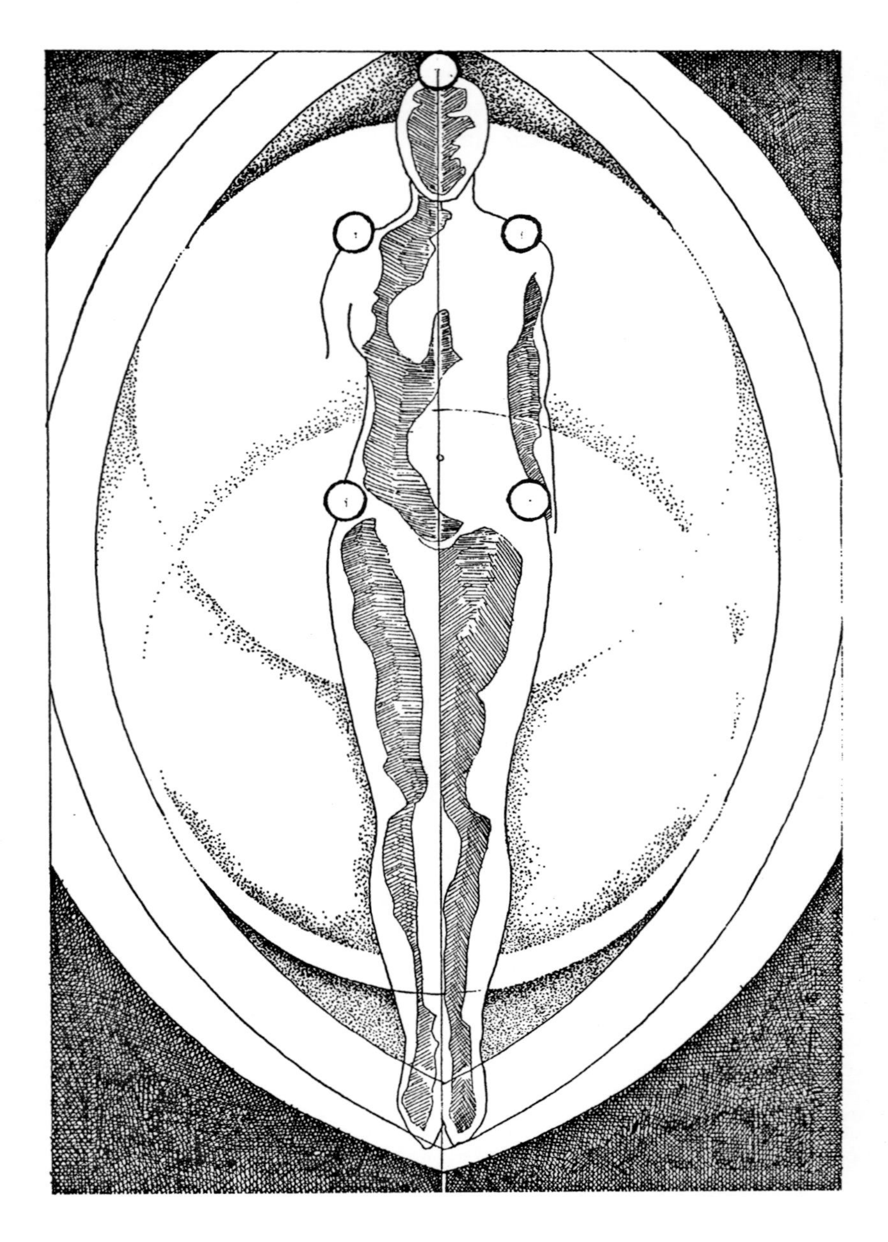

Moon net

Moon net

What you need

Five pieces of moonstone and a dark blue cloth. If there is one moonstone larger than the rest it is best placed at the top of the head. Two moonstones are placed in the hollows where the arms join the torso. Two are placed near the hipbones.

What this net can be used for

Soothing and calming the body and emotions; attunement to, and relief from, lunar influences; balancing physical problems in the digestive system and female reproductive organs.

This net is perhaps one of the most popular when demonstrated at workshops. There is often great reluctance to end the session, so comforted and nurtured one feels. It has been described like being wrapped in cotton wool, floating in moonlight, soothed and protected. Occasionally, as the body releases stress and adjusts to the energies, there may be a need to place a stone, such as turquoise or blue lace agate, at the throat to help ease feelings of pressure there.

Moonstone is a gem-quality variety of the mineral orthoclase and has long been admired for its beautiful soft luminescence and for its healing properties. In India it is the stone "par excellence" for women to wear. It has been found to calm the emotions and so is useful in times of stress and anxiety. In these circumstances it is the digestive system and solar plexus areas that tend to suffer first, and often, because the assimilation of nutrients is hampered, the skin accumulates toxins. Many skin conditions, as well as ulcers, are made worse by emotional factors, so the use of moonstone can be helpful with these conditions.

For those who wish to attune more closely to the energies of the moon this net is invaluable. The moon is our closest link to the solar system, the galaxy and the spaces beyond. It has become, as it were, a jumping off point both for internal and external exploration. It represents the hidden factors, the light that shines in the darkness, the reflection of those energies that cannot be looked at directly. Its link with the feminine and with the ocean tides is very clear. There has been enough experimentation to conclusively state that the lunar cycle effects every aspect of life on Earth, from the growth of plants, to the breeding cycles of animals, to birth, death and accident rates in humans. The subtle effects of gravitation and electromagnetic fields of the moon measure out time-cycles and the rhythms of all water-based life on this planet.

The cool radiance of the moon has been associated with the ambrosia of immortality and bliss. In Chinese legend there is not a man in the moon but a hare, symbol of liveliness and fertility, who pounds a pestle and mortar to produce the nectar of life. In Vedic India, Chandra, the moon, was associated with Soma, the food of the gods (a symbol for the subtle substance that sustains all aspects of creation), and was given the epithet "Indu", the drop. For those who might wish to come into closer contact with the moon energies, there is a mantra that can be used: AUM SOM SOMAYE NAMAH AUM.

Using a dark blue cloth creates a background energy of peacefulness and flow, a gentle amplification of the energy net itself.

Mercury net

What you need

A golden yellow cloth. Three citrine quartz and three clear quartz crystals. Hold the citrine crystals in each hand, points away from the body, and the third at the solar plexus, point down. The clear quartz is taped to the top of each foot between the second and third toes. The third clear quartz is placed in the centre of the forehead, point up towards the crown.

What this net can be used for

Linking to the energies of the planet Mercury; improvement of communication skills; adaptability; speed of thought; clarity of mind; balancing the left and right hemispheres of the brain.

Whereas other nets feel relaxing and comfortable the Mercury Net can sometimes be so activating that it becomes difficult to stay within the energies for more than a few moments. This can be the case when one is unfamiliar with this type of energy or if there is no need of further mental stimulation. If you are using this net to improve skills, start with regular short sessions and allow the time in the net to lengthen as you get acclimatised to the energy.

The stone placement here is important. Citrine at the solar plexus stimulates the major chakra in this area which activates the energy-producing ability of the physical system and the ability to receive and process information.

The citrine in the hands balances the subtle energy fields of the body and also the brain hemispheres which need to act coherently together for maximum efficiency. The quartz on the feet pointing downwards anchor the energy into the physical

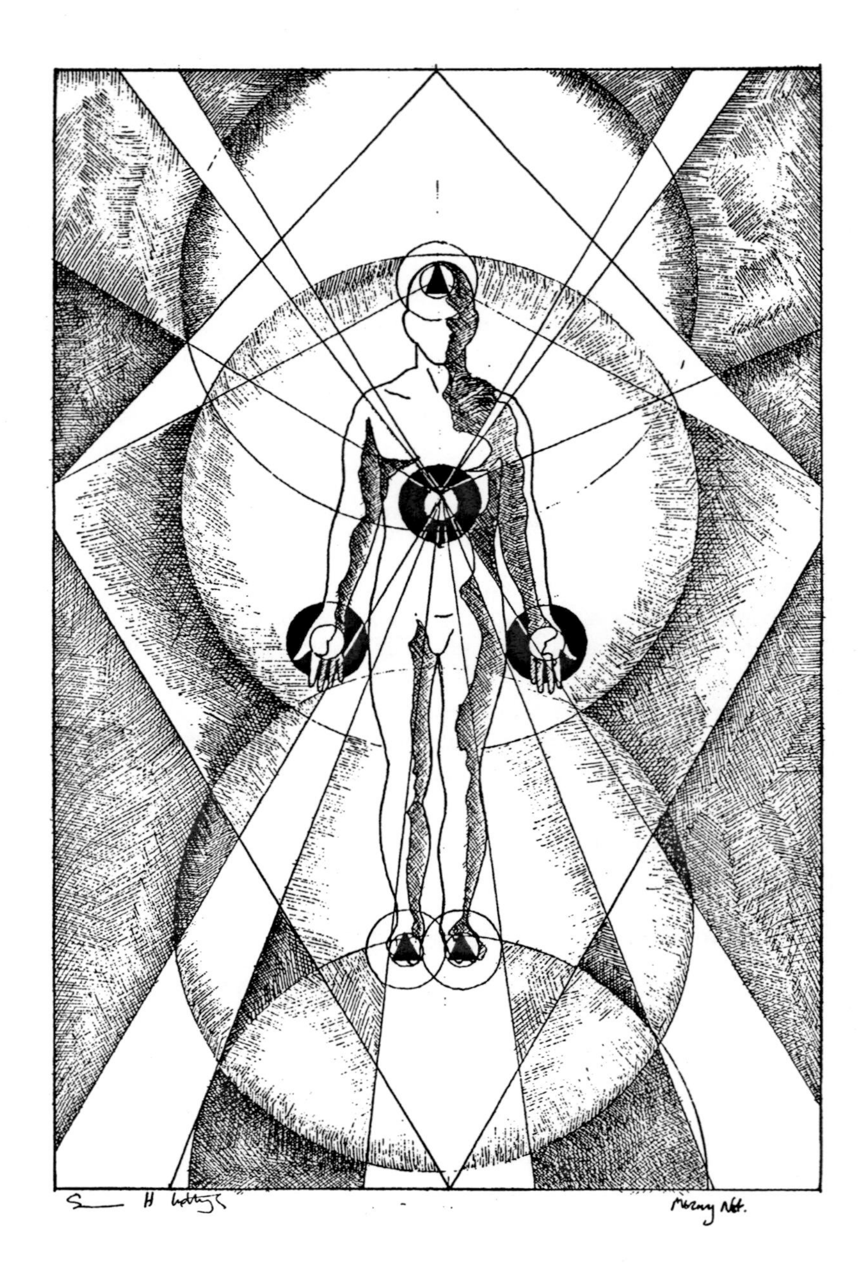

Mercury net

reality and allow the information received to be of practical value.The quartz on the forehead energises the brow chakra and thus mental functioning as a whole, particularly the clarity of perceptions.

When stones are placed both centrally and on either side of the body the nerve centres are stimulated to help balance the hemispheres of the brain, increasing the flow of energy, learning ability, balanced perception and physical co-ordination.

Mercury is the small planet closest to the sun, centre and controller of the solar system. Mercury functions as the messenger between the higher levels of creation, called by some "the gods", and the physical worlds with which we are familiar. The Roman god Mercury is the Greek god Hermes and the Egyptian Tehuti (Thoth), all famed for their cleverness, (if not guile and deceit!), and their ability to teach mankind new skills and new wisdom.

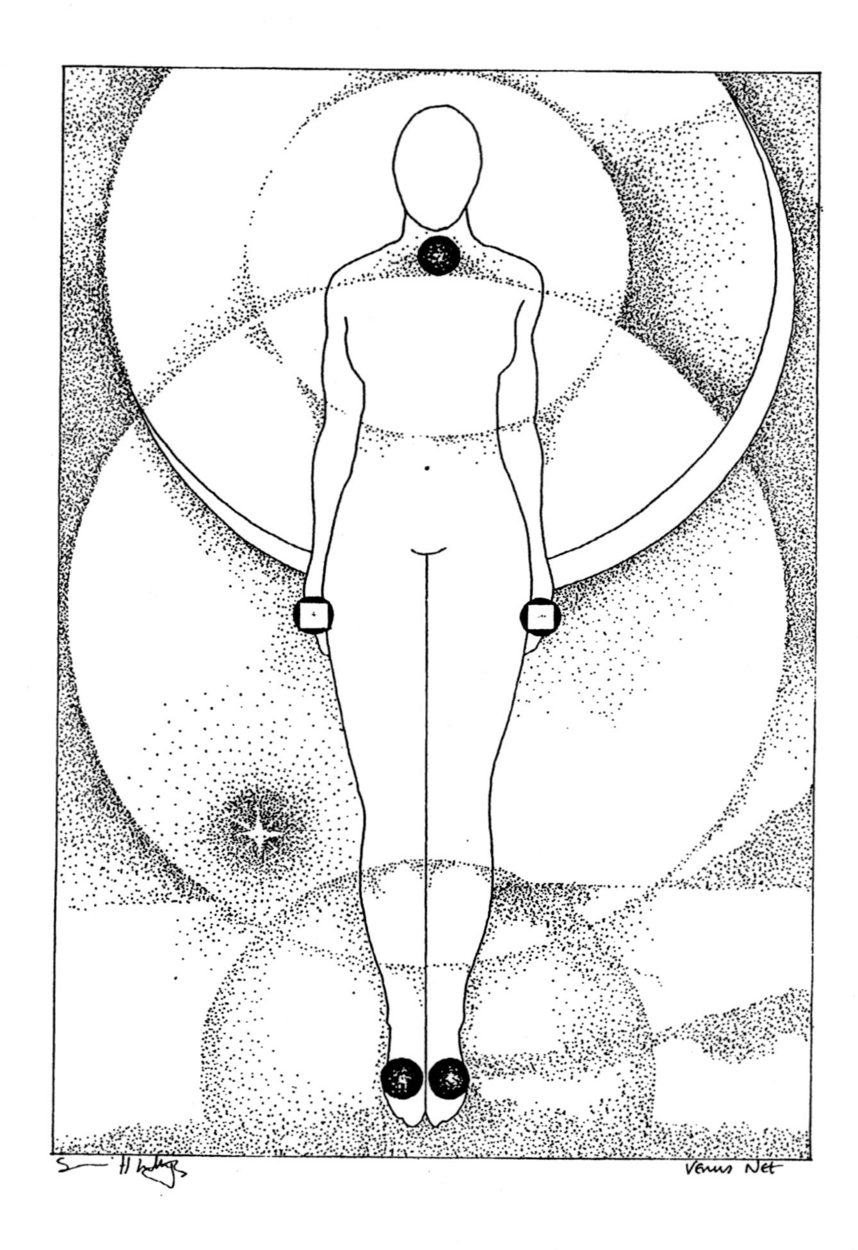

Venus net

Venus net

What you need

Three rose quartz, two clear quartz and a green cloth. All crystals are placed on the body. One rose quartz is at the base of the throat and the other two on the top of the feet between the tendons of the first and second toes. In either hand are the clear quartz with the terminated ends pointing away from the body.

What this net can be used for

Stimulating creativity and artistic abilities; increase of self-acceptance, self-worth and self-motivation; ability to relate to others; sexual tensions of any sort; attuning to the planet Venus.

The planet Venus has played important roles in many belief systems throughout the world. Apart from the sun and moon, Venus is the brightest object in our sky. Because it is so close to the sun, Venus is often seen as a bright forerunner just before sunrise and sunset. It is the Evening and Morning Star, Lucifer the Lightbringer. Many Central and South American temples were aligned to significant rising and setting points of this planet. In the Middle East the worship of the Evening and Morning Stars, seen as two twin gods, was closely related to the Mother Goddess religions from which much of the later Greek and Roman symbolism of Aphrodite and Venus arose. Aphrodite was in fact an import from the Levant via Cypress and derives her name from Ishtar and Astarte.

The name of Jerusalem probably means "*City of the god of the Evening Star*", the same god from whom the king Solomon took his name. Venus is usually associated with feminine energies, (even when portrayed by male deities, as in India), and the planet was linked to Isis and to Mary, Mother of God. So, there are hymns to the goddess as Morning Star in both later Egyptian and Christian religions. The aspects of the goddess rule all forms of bounteous giving, from the fertility of the Earth and its animals, through increase of harmony, pleasure and beauty, to the desire to attain to spiritual unity through integrating one's energies with "the other", whether that be as sexual love, artistic inspiration or exalted, Universal Love.

Like the Moon, which is also an aspect of the Mother Goddess, Venus appears to us in phases. In fact, the planet appears brightest to us when a crescent, as then it is much closer to the Earth than when it is full, around the far side of the sun.

Establishing a growing, harmonious relationship both within the Self and between the Self and others is a primary function of the heart chakra, and so it is appropriate that one of the major heart stones, rose quartz, belongs to the Venus net. It is no use feeling love, having ideas, getting inspired, if the energy can't flow from the heart to where it can be expressed through the throat chakra. Therefore, rose quartz placed at the throat will dissolve false or inappropriate inhibitions to true personal expression, and rose quartz at the feet will increase motivation and drive, as well as drawing up the naturally exuberant energy of the Earth.

Clear quartz, particularly terminated crystals, will help to remove and transmute the tensions released by the rose quartz and will bring clarity and strength to the auric field. Green is the traditional colour associated with Venus - linked to the metal copper and the colour that induces balance, harmony and growth.

Mars net

What you need

Nine clusters of clear quartz and a red cloth. The quartz clusters, which do not need to be large, are not to touch the body. One is placed above the head and the rest are evenly spaced with points outwards.

What this net can be used for

Motivation; strengthening of the ego and the will to do; removing blocks to progress, both internal and external; giving your energy a boost; increasing life-force; attuning to the planet Mars; reduction of aggression and tension; increase in libido.

Aggression has had a bad press. It is almost universally seen as a negative trait, something to be weeded out of the individual and out of society. But like every other human response and emotion, aggression has a positive as well as a negative face. Aggression is an expression of the desire for control, the desire to make one's own, to hold power, to win. All these are a means to grow. Aggression is one form of the primal energy of creation, which is the will to expand and to encompass. The problems arise when this force of will is used to gain personal power only, power that denies power to others. This is when aggression and the Mars energy becomes debased and open to the worst excesses of the ego.

Aggression wells up when one's own existence is perceived to be threatened in some way - when one's own power is under threat from someone else. As such it is an understandable survival response. In complex societies of the world today individual power has to a very large extent been removed in a

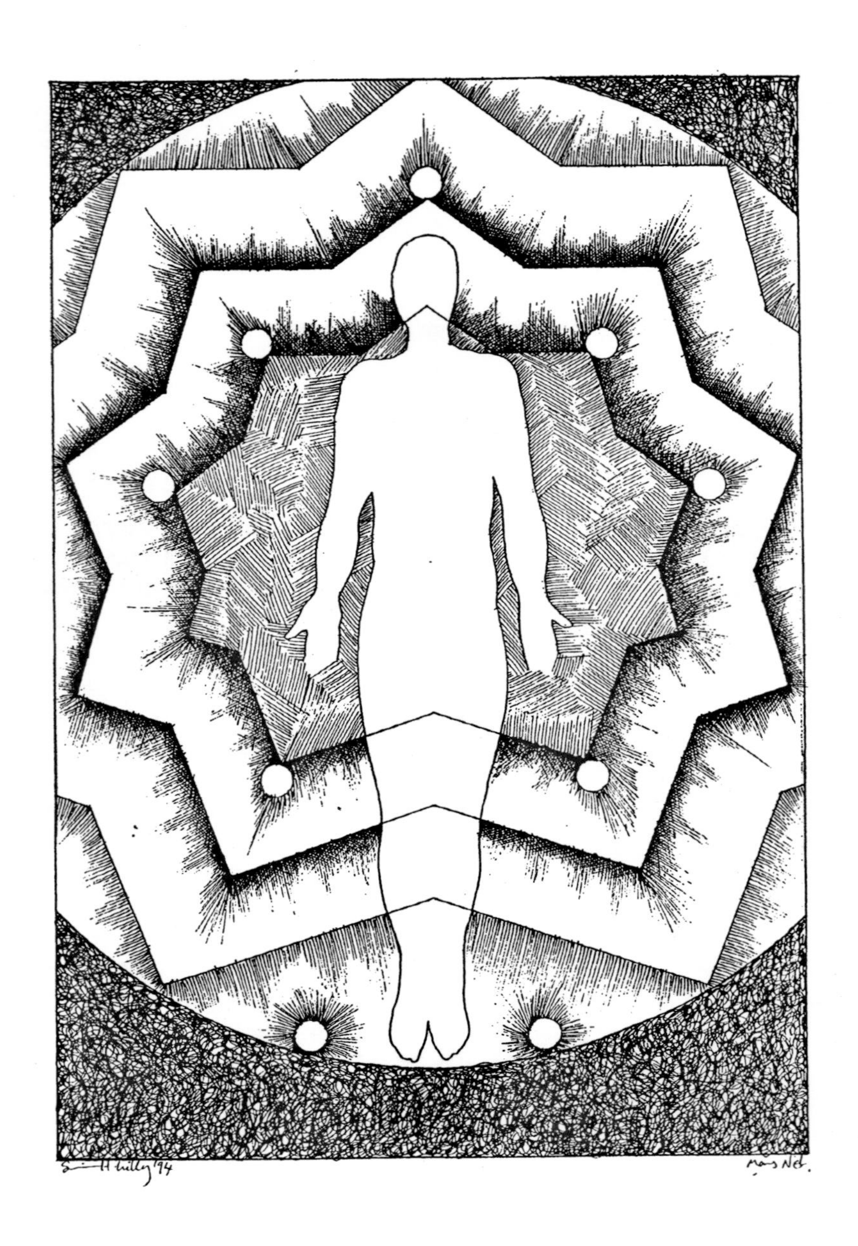

Mars net

forceful, if sometimes subtle, way by those groups or individuals who we seem to have elected for this very purpose. In some sense this amalgamation and centralisation of energy and information is a move towards a potential unification and evolutionary progress. But this progress can only be made if the unity comprises free individuals who are established in their own power, and thus of equal dignity and influence, not, as at present, the many being manipulated and milked of their power by a few who believe power is only control.

The rise of aggressive behaviour in these societies is perhaps merely a symptom of the lack of power many individuals feel. When there are limited means to express personal creativity or when creativity itself is seen as expendable or even as a threat to the status quo, the dynamic force of creation, symbolised by the planet Mars, flips over to reveal its other face, the dynamic force of destruction.

The Mars Net helps to balance these outward-going dynamic energies in a way which benefits both the individual and the environment. The dammed up energies which manifest as tension, frustration and aggression are given an outlet so that change can come about through creation rather than destruction. At the same time the influence of Mars can revitalise and stimulate one's own energies, empower the self with confidence and security and increase physical strength and stamina.

If you are dissatisfied, enervated, apathetic, hopeless, apologetic, constantly under the weather or fearful, if your life has lost its spark and direction, enter the Mars Net and ask yourself "To whom have I given my power?". When you find out, ask for that power to be returned to you.

Jupiter net

Jupiter net

What you need

Twelve clear quartz crystals and a blue cloth. If the quartz are terminated they are placed points outwards. One crystal is placed on the centre of the forehead while the remaining crystals are evenly spaced around the body.

What this net can be used for

Attuning to the planet Jupiter and its influences; understanding the laws of nature; spiritual, mental and physical expansion; openness to new concepts and images; understanding one's place in the universe; positivity, optimism and humour; urge to grow; opening doors.

Jupiter is the largest planet in the solar system, easily seen in the night sky without any telescope. Although of vast size it is composed mainly of gases and is less than a third of the earth's density. The gases of Jupiter rotate in coloured bands at different speeds giving it a beautiful, ever-changing and turbulently stormy appearance. Being the largest body in the universe after the sun Jupiter's gravitational influence is very important in the flow of energy within the solar system.

Jupiter's influence is in the area of growth of consciousness. It links us to the underlying energies (information = consciousness) of the universe, to a direct contact with the Universal Mind. Once in possession of this knowledge, even at a level below everyday awareness, we can begin to see how everything fits together, and this leads to a growing understanding of our life and its purpose.

Of course, once we have access to this level of awareness there will be a tendency to act in harmony with the flow of things (the Tao, or Way), and this means that our needs are met with less effort expended on our part. The nature of life is to gather more and more, and this too is the nature of Jupiter's influence - limitless expansion, questing beyond established boundaries, growth. When it is out of balance this can lead to excesses of greed and the need to acquire on many different levels, be it food, information, pleasure or riches.

The Jupiter Net helps with a proper balance of growth and an increased ability to contact the True or Higher Self. It can help to give understanding to the "whys?" of any situation and can ensure a more positive approach to life. If you fear loss of any kind, if you lack abundance in your life, if your sense of humour has deserted you, the Jupiter Net will help restore your links with the Universal flow.

The centre of the forehead is close to where the chakra commonly called the third eye is found. This energy centre's main function is perception - understanding and making sense of what the eyes see, the senses experience and what the mind thinks. The brow chakra integrates this information and allows a new light of understanding to flower. Metaphor, analogy, "gestalt", visions and dream images are the means of transmitting this language of light to the conscious awareness. The power of symbols and ritual arise from this interface of the higher mind with the physical. Placing a crystal quartz on this point and also surrounding the body is a bit like opening the eyes and being able to see not just in front of you but all around 360 degrees. One sees oneself in a new light.

Saturn net

What you need

Four clear quartz crystals and four rose quartz. A pink cloth. All stones are on the body, points inwards. One clear quartz at the centre of the forehead, one in either hand, one at the centre of the pubic bone. All rose quartz are taped to the feet, between the tendons of the first and second toe and between the tendons of the second and third toes. It is best to use fairly small, light pieces of rose quartz here!

What this net can be used for

Patience; self-discipline; establishing foundations; understanding the processes of Time; practicality; strength to fulfil one's goals; easing problems related to Saturn transits; understanding and removing blocks to progress; fulfilment of desires.

Saturn, the ringed planet, is even less dense than Jupiter, but although twice as far from the Earth as that planet, it is so large that it can be seen with the naked eye. Saturn is the outermost of the ancient world's solar system and so is regarded as a bridge between the material, everyday awareness and the mysterious worlds of higher consciousness.

Superficially, Saturn seems to be bad news when it trundles through an astrological chart, bringing restriction, contraction and a slowing down of all processes to its own slow pace. It is Old Father Time, inexorably cutting a swathe through dreams of success and ambition. It is Satan, the Tempter, who puts problems in the way, who delays and brings apparent bad luck. ("luck" derives from the name of the Norse trickster god Loki who causes mischief and harm wherever possible). Saturn is a

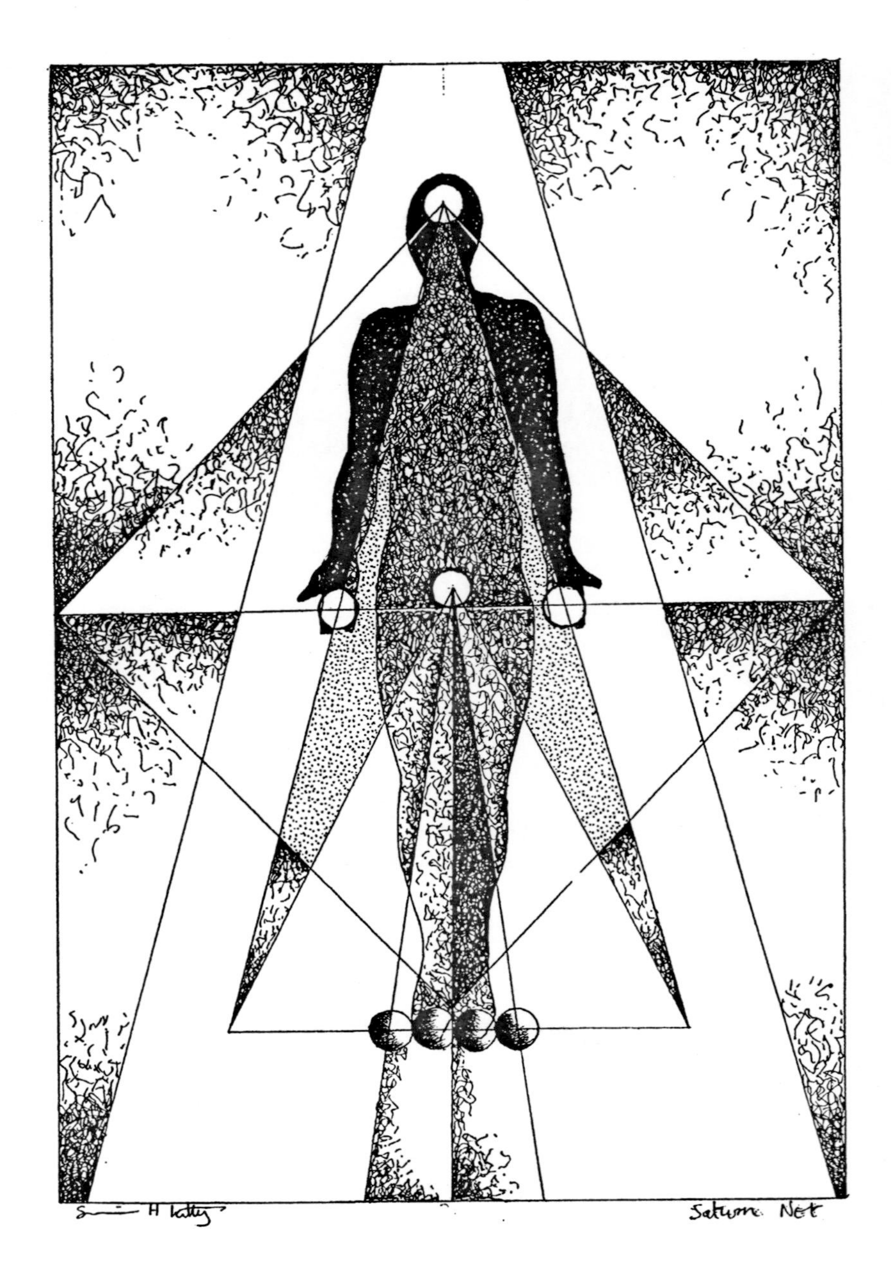

Saturn net

spoilsport. Saturn acts by preventing us from wasting our time in hedonistic, short-sighted and egotistical pursuits. It helps us to move beyond self-centred adolescence to a more stable, fruitful growth. In this way Saturn is the sober guardian who can balance the excesses of an exuberant Jupiter.

Saturn and its influence can never be hurried because its energies are to do with establishing strong foundations which take time and patience. There are no short cuts to personal growth. The paradox is that self-discipline, practicality and patience are essential in order to grow to a state where the Self has freedom from time and space. Depending on one's perception, Saturn is either the creator of obstacles or the remover of limitations. In truth, what we decide to do with these energies is up to us, but Saturn will never let us out of the classroom until we have completed and learned the lessons we need to be truly free.

Whenever we are facing a brick wall in life, when there seems to be an insurmountable obstacle, when every way one turns leads to more problems, when one is bogged down in minutiae and restricted, when one's goals seem impossibly far away and when one feels burdened down with responsibilities and obligations, that is the time to enter the Saturn Net. Here you will find clues to the lessons that have to be learned and how to complete them. Bear in mind when you enter the net the nature of the obstacle and be open to what comes to you. Remember that even something which may appear to be an outside influence over which you have no control, (ie "It's not my fault that...."), is still able to be altered, though it may be you that needs to change rather than the situation. If you can't climb the brick wall Saturn may give you the directions to walk around it or even find a doorway where you hadn't thought of looking.

The stones for this net emphasise the grounding, practical earthing nature of the Saturn energies - activating the perceptions with quartz at the brow whilst establishing the energy in the root chakra and in the motivating energies of the hands and feet. The pink cloth and rose quartz reveal that the only limitations are the ones we place upon ourselves by choosing to turn away from what we can be. The pink re-emphasises the acceptance and understanding of the Self as a whole, integrated, worthy being, equal and united to everything else in creation. Saturn limits us until we learn that the only freedom from all limitations is love itself.

Uranus net

What you need

Six small clear quartz clusters to be placed on the body. Six green stones such as emerald, aventurine, malachite, dioptase. A pink cloth. A small quartz cluster is placed on the forehead; two in the hollows by the shoulders (the coracoid processes); two resting near the hip-bones, and the last in the centre of the pubic bone. The green stones are placed above the head and below the feet and evenly spaced around the body.

What this net can be used for

For those who are rebels, uncomfortable with the usual patterns of society; increasing group awareness; intuition and invention; new ideas; awakening higher consciousness; over-sensitivity to electromagnetic influences; new ways out of old situations; illumination.

Uranus was first discovered by William Herschel in 1781. Only the invention of the telescope made it possible to see this planet, which is 1.7 billion miles from the Earth. Uranus is a huge, green planet composed mainly of water and gas, and is the third largest planet in the solar system. It is the only planet that has an axis of tilt almost 100 degrees to the plane of its orbit.

While the seven inner planets affect the individual in a personal way, the three outer planets mainly influence humanity as a whole, bringing about shifts of consciousness and evolutionary change. Uranus presents two characteristics. It is the bringer of group awareness, of an expansion of consciousness beyond personal concerns and desires, while at the same time bringing flashes of intuition and invention and

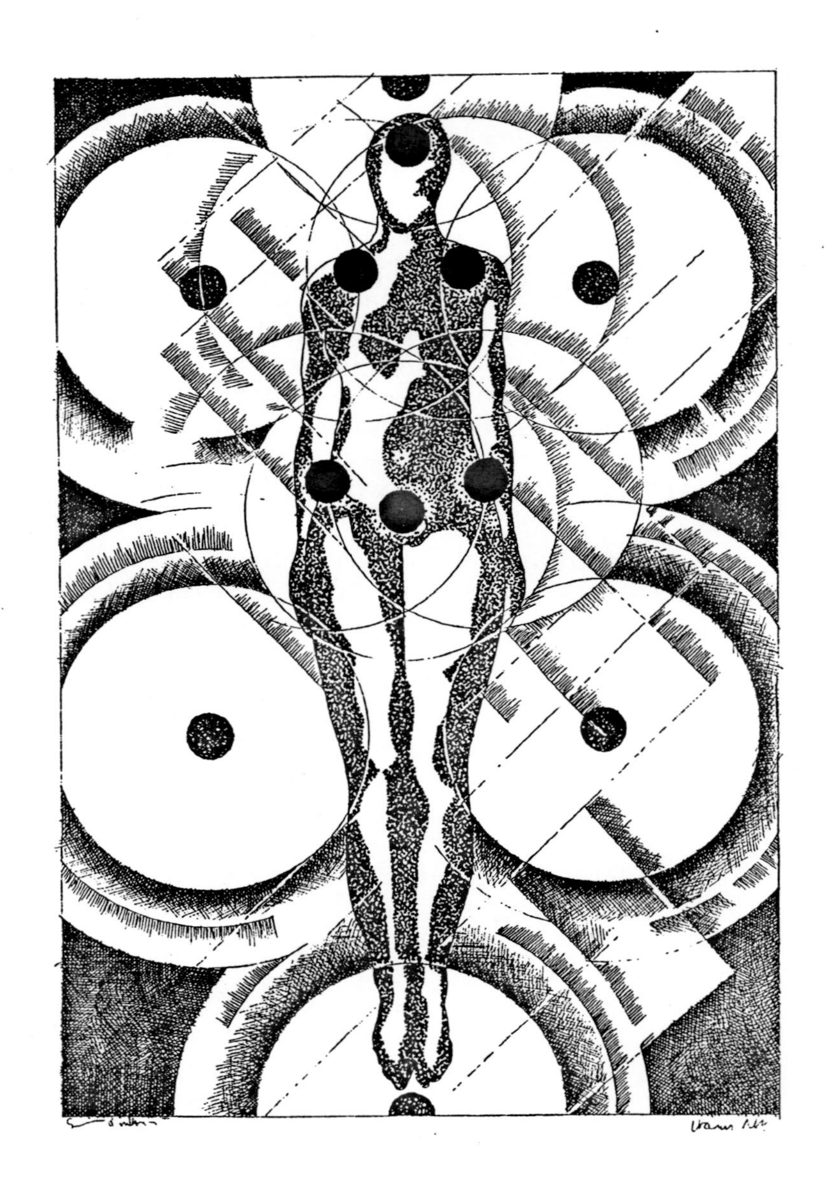

Uranus net

encouraging unorthodox, independent behaviour. Uranus pushes us beyond our nice, neat boundaries. It opens up new possibilities and destroys old certainties and structures. If anyone is stuck in a negative Saturn mode - hidebound, restricted, dogmatic, refusing to shift ground - Uranus is the anarchist's bomb, the streaker across the cricket pitch, the quantum leap of awareness, the bolt of lightning that awakens higher consciousness, new possibilities and the awareness of wonderful futures.

We have noticed that those people who are very sensitive to electricity and electromagnetic energy in such a way as to make them open to chronic energy loss or constant infection nearly always have a sensitively placed Uranus in their natal chart. Those subject to a build-up of static electricity, who have consistent problems with electrical appliances, who find travelling in cars, lifts, or being near large metal surfaces disturbing, who find thunderstorms physically uncomfortable, or those who work in high electromagnetic fields like computers, microwave ovens and telecommunications, are all likely to have this problem.

Of course, these days we are living, or almost drowning, in a sea of electromagnetic radiations. This tends to change the natural resonances of the cells and molecular activities of the body, which puts the physical system under enormous stress. The Uranus Net can help to reduce or remove this "entrainment" to electrical resonance and restore a more normal electrical environment. This net will also balance those who are full of nervous energy or who are hyperactive, acting like a lightning conductor to draw the excess away to the ground.

The quartz crystals balance the body polarities - the negative and positive charges of the physical system - while the green stones help balance the subtle bodies and calm excess activity.

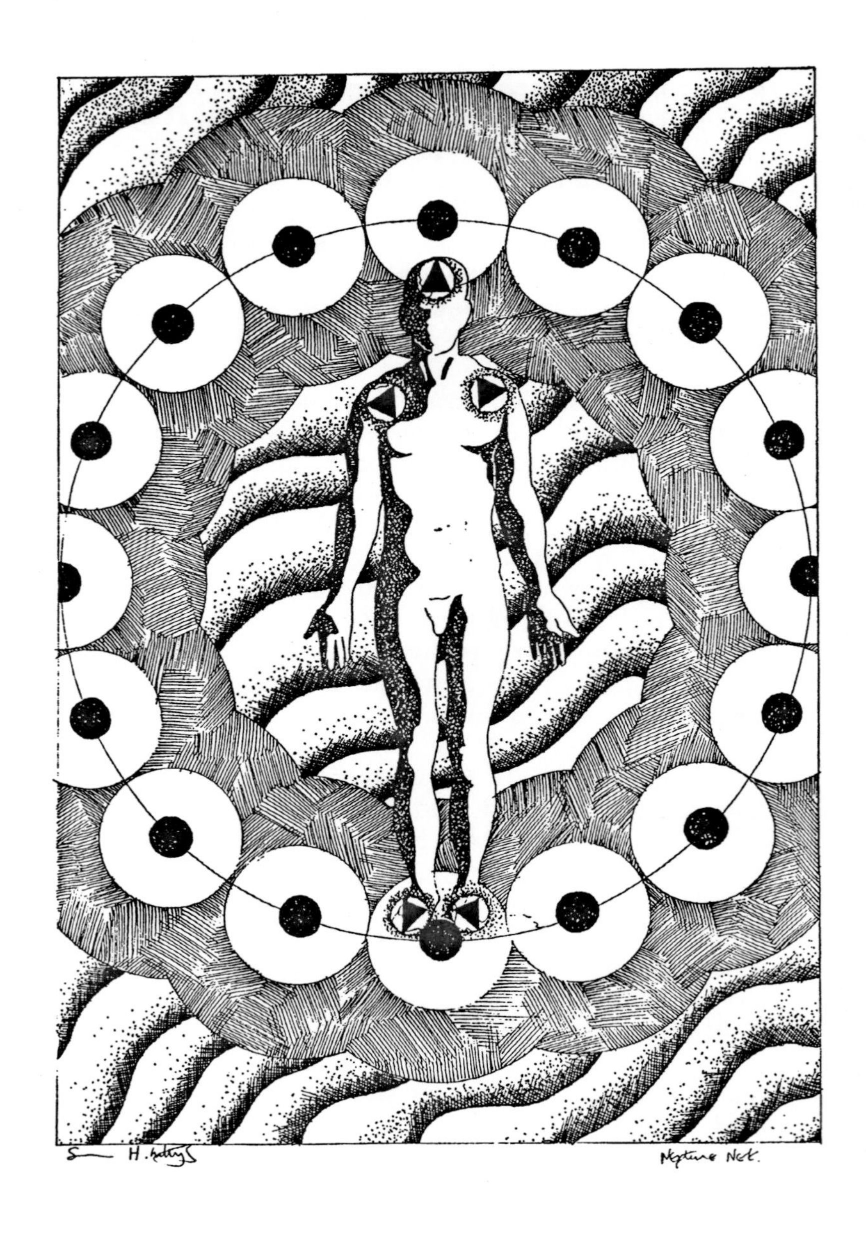

Neptune net

Neptune net

What you need

A blue cloth. Five smoky quartz crystals and sixteen pieces of natural chalk. The chalk is evenly spaced around the body. The smoky quartz is placed as follows: all crystals point away from the throat; two are placed at the coracoid processes by the shoulders with points facing outwards from the base of the throat; two crystals are placed between the first and second toes on both feet; one smoky quartz is placed just below the crown on the back of the head, known as the bindu point.

What this net can be used for

Inspiration; encouraging true psychic visions and clairvoyance; creative imagination; exploring the boundless aspects of creation; transforming negative tendencies such as laziness, self-indulgence, addictions, fantasy; obsessions and phobias; attuning to finer aspects of universal love and cosmic tides.

Whilst Uranus is the higher vibration of Mercury dealing with mind and the communication of ideas or energy, Neptune is the higher vibration of Venus - the emotions. With Neptune personal love and the joy of sharing has the chance to expand into a universal love of giving. This openness allows inspiration and mystical truths to take shape through one's emotional creativity. However, Neptune is a tricky, Will-of-the-Wisp energy to get hold of, as the means of its discovery suggests.

At the beginning of the nineteenth century it was noticed that Uranus was not behaving quite as predicted and this led to the mathematical supposition of a further, invisible planet that was influencing the gravitational field of Uranus. Eventually, in 1846, Johann Galle, a German astronomer visually located the new planet which was named Neptune after its blue-green colour. Neptune is completely invisible to the naked eye and, although similar in structure to Uranus, is a billion miles further from the Earth.

In its finest manifestation Neptune is the instigator of inspiration, particularly music and dance, and the mystic arts: inspired writings,visions, clairvoyance, cosmic truths and so on. However, because the energies are so subtle and unearthly there is a tendency to get carried away in the realms of fantasy and escapism, and this tends to get things very fuzzy and unclear - the boundaries between what is and what is not become difficult to discern. This is where we are contacting energies as they emerge and differentiate from the underlying ocean of the Absolute. Because we have a tendency to live in an ego-centred world of perception when we are faced with a non-personalised, non-individualised view of things we can easily lose our way: nothing has familiar labels, "things" as such melt away into mystery. Neptune is similar to the Egyptian goddess Nebet Het (Nepthys to the Greeks), the hidden side of the feminine, watery energies, the hidden mystery which cannot be defined or pinned down.

Use the Neptune Net to tune to the finer levels of this planet's influence and to transform the negative tendencies. If there is a desire to withdraw from the world and its responsibilities into escapism or fantasy; if you are tending towards destructive, self-indulgent habit patterns such as alcohol or other drugs; if you are becoming a selfish, lazy slob (either in your own or other's eyes!), or if you suffer from phobias or obsessions, turn the Neptune energy to better use - instead of dissolving into boundless unconsciousness yourself bring the mystery out and express it in a practical way.

The stones for this net are peculiar and particular. The five smoky quartz act as an anchor back into the solid, physical reality and direct the expressive, creative energy of the throat chakra outwards to all parts of the body. Smoky quartz is an expression of the hidden unmanifest aspects of creation, the absorption of light, in contrast to clear quartz's reflection of light. Smoky quartz is introvertive, revealing hidden depths, very protecting and cleansing, and as such is useful for meditative states. The bindu point on the back of the head, just behind the crown, symbolises the first manifestation of the universe ("bindu" meaning "point"), and is the link to that state where everything exists in union. The chalk pieces around the body recall images of long dead sea creatures whose shells took the spiral forms of growth found throughout the universe, from DNA to galaxies, and whose element was the watery ocean, the Sea of Becoming, ruled over by the god of the sea, Neptune.

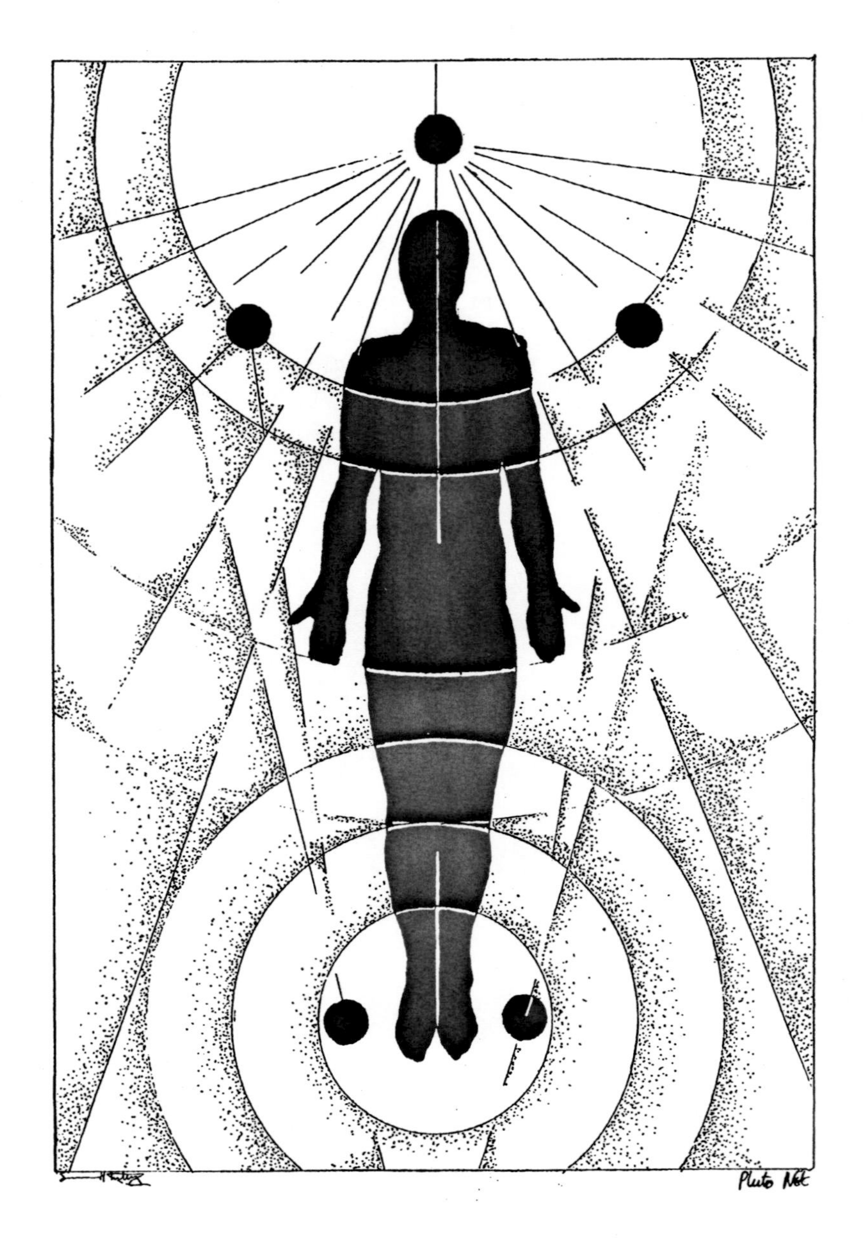

Pluto net

Pluto net

What you need

Five pieces of dark obsidian, a black or red cloth. One obsidian is placed above the head; one piece either side of the shoulder-neck area; one to the outside of each foot.

What this net can be used for

Difficult Pluto aspects and Pluto transits; bringing hidden things to light; linking with the unconscious; renewal of the lifeforce; understanding and experiencing the processes of life and death; deep cleansing and purification; breaking out of inhibitions and inappropriate behaviour patterns.

Pluto is the outermost planet of the solar system so far discovered, (a tenth planet has been postulated but not located). Pluto has an irregular orbit which sometimes takes it closer to the sun than Neptune, but on average is 3,666 billion miles from the sun. It was discovered in 1930 following unexplained irregularities in Uranus's orbit - Pluto effects the gravitational fields and motions of both Uranus and Neptune. Pluto is a very small planet the size of our moon, probably composed of ice and methane.

Pluto was named after the Roman god of the Underworld (sometimes confused with another god,Plutus, god of wealth), and it is interesting to see the synchronicity of its discovery with world events. At this time arose the turmoil of the rise of Nazism, the Second World War, the development of atomic power and the creation of this planet's namesake, plutonium.

The principal function of Pluto is the transformation of energy from the very deepest levels outwards. Its action is supremely cleansing and redeeming, but not something you would wish on a friend! Pluto strips away everything that is no longer necessary. It is an annihilator and eliminator of dross and imperfection. Trying to prevent the action of Pluto is like trying to avoid the inevitability of death, or like trying to stop a train at full speed by standing on the track and refusing to move! It may seem like a good idea at the time - but it doesn't work. Pluto will regenerate, it will reveal suppressed and unconscious energies, it will reveal imperfections and inhibitions, and its effects will not go away until there has been the acceptance that a complete renewal is necessary and is the only way forward. The influence of a powerful Pluto transit can be a good practice run for death itself - and, in fact, if the influence of Pluto is resisted, death on one level or another is what will occur.

Pluto is the power of Siva, the overwhelming Ocean of Being which has its two tides of creation and destruction, and which moves according to its own dance. It is the understanding of the reality that growth means change from one state to another - definitions of life and death are impositions of the scared, limited ego-consciousness which fears to lose the shell giving it shape and yet cannot grow any further without casting off the shell and growing another larger home.

Pluto's influence is a manifestation of the greater universal tide. The best way to cope with it is not to resist in any way, because that resistance is against the flow of life itself. Acceptance and understanding of the processes of death and the ability to let go of established notions of who you think you are, eases the growth process that Pluto initiates.

Obsidian is volcanic glass. As such it is closely associated with the Underworld and those things that are thrown up into daylight from the unseen realms. Created by massive heat, obsidian is also linked with the fires of transformation and purification. Obsidian is a stone for connecting with the core energies of the planet, and it is protecting, grounding and stabilising. It also has the ability of bringing to awareness those aspects of ourselves that need changing. In this and in other ways, such as the traditional use of an obsidian mirror for scrying or seeing visions, obsidian reveals the underlying reality of any situation. So in this net obsidian roots us into the Earth's own energies whilst allowing us to understand and process the transformative vibrations of Pluto.

Chiron net

Chiron net

What you need

Six pieces of turquoise and a yellow cloth. One stone is placed above the head and below the feet, either side of the shoulders and either side of the thighs, just by the hands.

What this net can be used for

Deep belief systems; fundamental blocks to development; buried hurts; "chip on the shoulder"; hidden skills developed for growth; releases from the past; courage to make changes to life; resolving difficulties from the past; giving a breathing space to make re-evaluations and find insight.

Chiron is a small planetoid about four hundred miles in diameter with an eccentric orbit which at times crosses the paths of Saturn and Uranus. It was discovered in 1977 and has been associated with major changes in education and healing.

The mythical being Chiron was the first centaur, half man-half horse, who was born in a cave where he spent most of his life as a teacher and foster-parent to many Greek heroes. He was famed for teaching the arts of music, ethics, astrology, healing, hunting and war.

Chiron was accidentally wounded by a poisoned arrow, which for all his skill he was unable to heal. Because Chiron was immortal he could not die but continued to suffer in pain. Finally he offered his life in exchange for the freeing of Prometheus from his punishment of unending torture given to him by the gods for going against their wishes in showing mankind how to make and use fire.

This myth helps to show us the influence that the planetoid Chiron has on humanity. The centaur is half man and half animal and so links us to Nature and towards a new sense of wholeness in the world. Once this is achieved we too can become master healers and skilled in the arts of living. However, Chiron remains hidden away within his cave - pupils come to him to learn. The potential for wholeness is hidden in the unconscious depths of ourselves. It must be actively sought out and worked with to be of any use. Chiron is to do with following one's own path to wholeness, to go it alone when necessary, to quest for the key that will give us access to the wholeness we desire.

Chiron is the wounded healer within us all. At those special times when Chiron becomes active in our lives we have the opportunity to face and overcome the very deepest hurts, the wounds we let nobody, not even ourselves, see, which are the very things preventing us from achieving our goals. These wounds can be the most fundamental concepts or belief systems that we each hold as defining what we are and what we are able to achieve. It is easy to forget that we have created who we are by recognising or choosing who we are not. "I'm not like that!" defines us as much as "That's me!". The mass of denials and negative choices is the exact mirror image of our conscious personalities. It is what Jung termed the Shadow - the unlit area created by the solidity of our "real" selves, which is an undeniable part of our energies. If we exist, we cast shadows - we cannot exist without both parts.

The Shadow is not by any means all negative or "bad", for it represents those paths we have not taken, those choices we have not made, those skills we have not developed. Where we are feeble, scared and inadequate, our Shadow is strong, brave and supremely confident (and, of course, vice versa!).

It takes a lot of psychic energy to maintain our conscious selves, and it takes much more energy to keep the Shadow self hidden in its cave of the unconscious. Proceeding with great caution it is possible, and desirable, to begin to integrate and use the Shadow, freeing up the enormous amounts of energy locked there.

While Chiron cannot be linked to the Shadow in all its actions, it is the means by which new doors can be opened, and old wounds that we have refused to see healed can begin to be honestly dealt with. Chiron gives us the opportunity to take a step towards wholeness and integration. It is the teacher and the healer within us all. And no-one knows better what we need to learn and what we need to heal than ourselves.

Turquoise is a beautiful stone used in many cultures of the world for thousands of years for its healing and spiritual properties. It is almost universally used as a protective amulet and in fact turquoise does seem to strengthen all the energy systems of the body, both physical and subtle. The colour specifically activates communication skills, creativity and intuition, and the combination of blue and green has a particularly energising effect on the thymus gland between the heart and throat which is so important for the health of the immune system. Turquoise is the stone of the sky, found within the earth - it brings together and blends the physical and the spiritual and so is an ideal stone for the integration and healing the Chiron Net requires. Yellow is the colour of integration and assimilation, and also joy and contentment, giving a safe, sunny space in which to heal those deep hurts and illuminate the darkest corners of ourselves with a positive light.

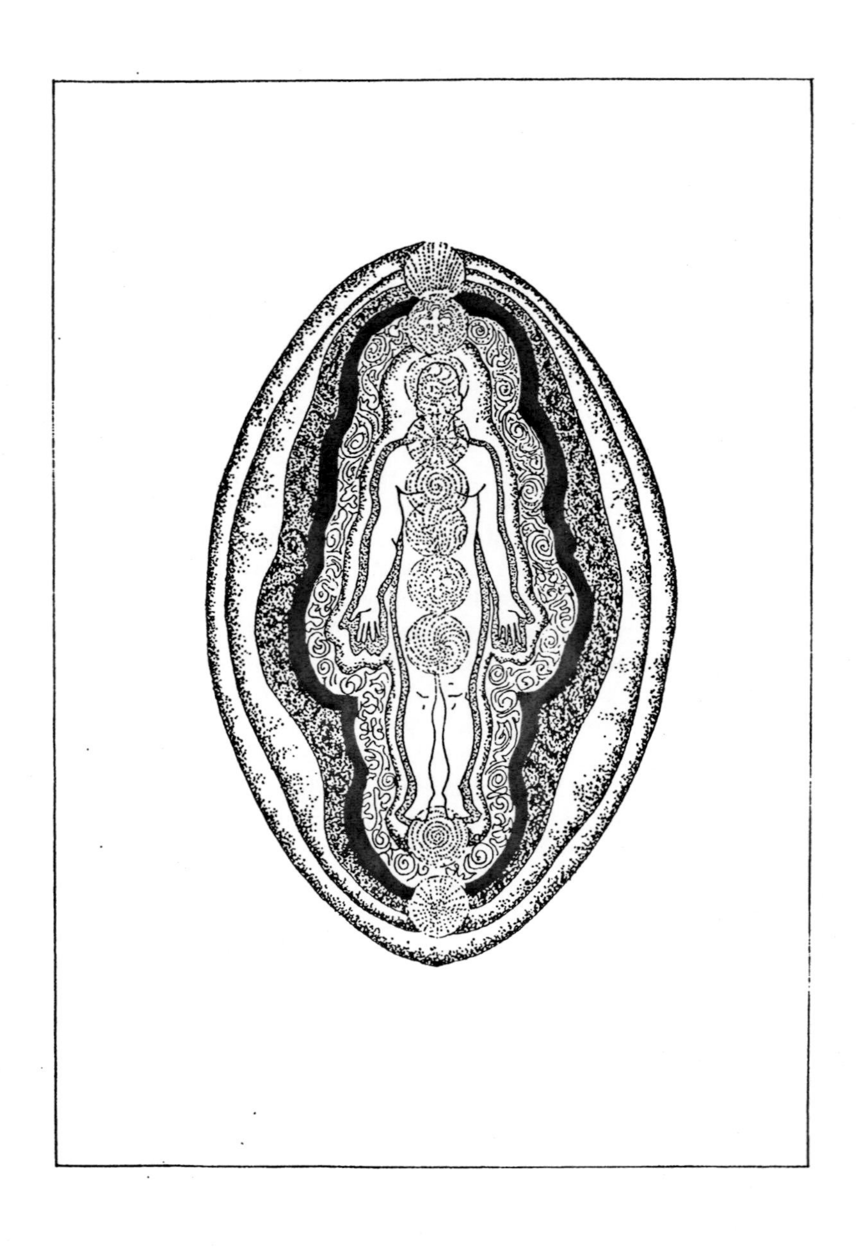

The Self nets

Introduction to nets of the self

This series of nets focuses on broadening and clarifying awareness of who we are and what we can achieve. Don't expect to come to any firm conclusions - rather be prepared for an expanding of possibilities, an inkling of "other things going on."

The nature of the Self and how it is seen and understood, like the nature of the Solar System, depends very much on the perspective of the viewer.

Cultural definitions of the Self vary enormously: from a here-and-now personality make-up, strictly within the physical boundary of the body, to a luminous spiritual entity, free of time and space, that permeates all existence yet focuses locally in a physical form. Most cultures agree that there is more to a person than a physical body and what can be perceived solely with the five senses.

Existing as we do in a culture that habitually looks outwards, and tends to feel uneasy about any sort of introspection, most of us have little idea of how to go about turning our attention inwards.

Like exploring the ocean, we can start from the shore that we know and gradually wade out acclimatising to new conditions. Once we get past a certain point, however,the familiar becomes the unknown, and we need to have some idea of how to cope. The first point to hold in mind is that there seems to be a lot more of the unconscious - that of which we are not usually consciously aware - than the conscious mind. Returning to the imagery of the sea: it is as though the conscious waking mind is the foam on a wave-top while the wave itself and the depth of water moving beneath it is the underlying nature of the Self.

Living as we do in the conditions of "wave-top" we are very conscious of our physical boundaries, our relationships in space and time and how we are in contrast to all the other individual waves around us.

Should we turn our attention away from our sense experiences downwards into the body of our wave and deeper into the water beneath we would find our sense of "us", the sense of individual identity, of "self", beginning to change. As awareness focuses into the wave we find that it extends further out and deeper than our usual perceptions allow. We are able to experience more of time and space - more of the direction in which the wave that is "us" is travelling and more of the direction from where we have come - the past. In other words, our knowledge has expanded. What may be difficult at this stage is that we are no longer experiencing in familiar ways - in the body of the wave there is no feeling of air or wind and the play of light is different. The unfamiliar may be confusing unless we allow ourselves to experience in different ways - exploring the Self needs flexibility, curiosity, openness and a certain caution - but there is no place for fear. We are, after all, exploring home territory. Unless we learn to feel safe in ourselves we cannot hope to feel secure in any other circumstance. Equally until we have explored as much of ourselves as we can we will not be able to know what is possible for us to achieve.

The wave may be a big, exciting place to the foam-fleck of conscious awareness but it does have some boundaries, albeit much larger ones. When our awareness dives into the ocean beneath the waves, boundaries expand so quickly it may appear that none exist. Here is where panic can set in. The "Self" suddenly seems to encompass other waves, other currents, different times, different places and can seem to be in several "places" at the same "time". Where fundamental patterns of belief systems (the idiosyncratic rules of what is real and what is not) are called into question, it is more comfortable to accept that ALL experience is valid.

Make notes, record the experience and allow it a lot of time to find a comfortable spot in your mind. Not everything makes sense, but it can still be real.

Problems can arise when unthought-of possibilities are denied or dismissed out-of-hand. Denial undermines the basis of experience. The mind tell you something happened, you deny that event, your mind begins to doubt itself, confusion increases and a lot of energy is caught up unnecessarily in sweeping things under the carpet and making sure they don't creep out while you're not looking. This way lies insanity. Avoid it whenever possible by employing amused neutrality, detached curiosity, a sense of humour and the sure knowledge that you will never comprehend everything in the universe.

Personal potential net

Activating personal potential net

What you need

A yellow cloth, five rose quartz and five clear quartz. All the rose quartz are placed in contact with the body, if they are pointed crystals the terminations are inwards. One is placed at the crown of the head; one in each hand and one on each foot between the tendons of the first and second toes. The five clear quartz are placed around the body - on either side of the head, either side of the legs at about knee level, and one beneath the feet. All points are inwards.

What this net can be used for

Clearing emotional blocks; cleansing and healing; helping to develop suppressed or diverted skills; self-development and integration.

This net is indicated when there is a feeling of confusion and a lack of direction. It helps to remove the accumulated debris from our windows of perception so that we are able to see more clearly. The placement of crystals creates two intersecting pentagrams of rose and clear quartz, which together make up a ten-pointed star.

The pentagram and the number five represents the world of matter in which we dwell, our physical bodies and the laws and substances from which they are made. Five stands midway between zero and ten, between matter and spirit. It is harmony and balance, controlled by the laws of an orderly universe. Ten is completion, the union of spirit and matter, body and soul, the bringing down of the highest into the lowest, the anchoring of all-that-is into the here-and-now. Ten is the number of the Earth itself.

The rose quartz, clear quartz and yellow cloth unite to remove misunderstandings and align our physical, emotional and mental selves, helping to bring the recognition of who we are and what it is possible to achieve.

Clarification on all levels

What you need

Five clear quartz crystals, two rubies or two topaz, one moldavite and one black tourmaline. A green cloth. All the quartz are in contact with the body, points inwards. One is placed at the crown of the head, one in each hand and one on each foot. The two rubies (or topaz), are placed side by side below the feet. The black tourmaline is placed away from the body at about knee level on the left side. The moldavite is put on the right side of the body opposite the tourmaline.

What this net can be used for

When there is a situation or an issue of which you wish to have a greater understanding; helps to remove energies that are clouding the true nature of things.

This net can be used for internal clarity, like an occasional spring-clean of the subtle energy fields, or for bringing clarity to some external situation. With the latter it is best to enter the net with the issue firmly in mind, gently mull over the circumstances, then relax and see what insights emerge. Even if there is no obvious shift of perspective you will probably find that you are better able to handle difficult situations in your everyday life.

Clear quartz energises and cleanses the aura and helps to realign subtle energy patterns when they have become muddled. This misalignment can occur after a shock or accident, or when there is emotional upset. Most frequently these days it results from overexposure to manmade electromagnetic fields such as high-tension power cables, very high or very low frequency transmitters, radar, microwave towers,

Clarification on all levels

underground cables and pipes, computers and fluorescent light. All these tend to superimpose their frequency patterns on our body's own, natural electromagnetic fields and if we become overexposed, especially when we are rundown, we can suffer from energy entrainment that creates stress at every level, from the molecular functioning of the cell to our behaviour patterns. There is now a growing body of evidence that clearly implicates artificial electromagnetic radiations in a wide range of dysfunctions and disease.

Rubies and topaz are both very good energisers and placed by the feet they emphasise earthing and grounding effects, which are essential to avoid build-up of unnecessary "static" energy within the body. This pathway to earth is like a lightning conductor. If you find yourself in a stressful situation it is often very helpful to "pull the plug" and allow all the excess emotions, thoughts and feelings to slide away through you into the earth where they can be safely neutralised.

Moldavite and black tourmaline are both excellent protectors from external influences and provide a link both to earth and to the cosmos. The green cloth provides space for your own energy systems to regain balance and calm, and like the rubies and moldavite, cleanse and balance the heart through which all truth is perceived.

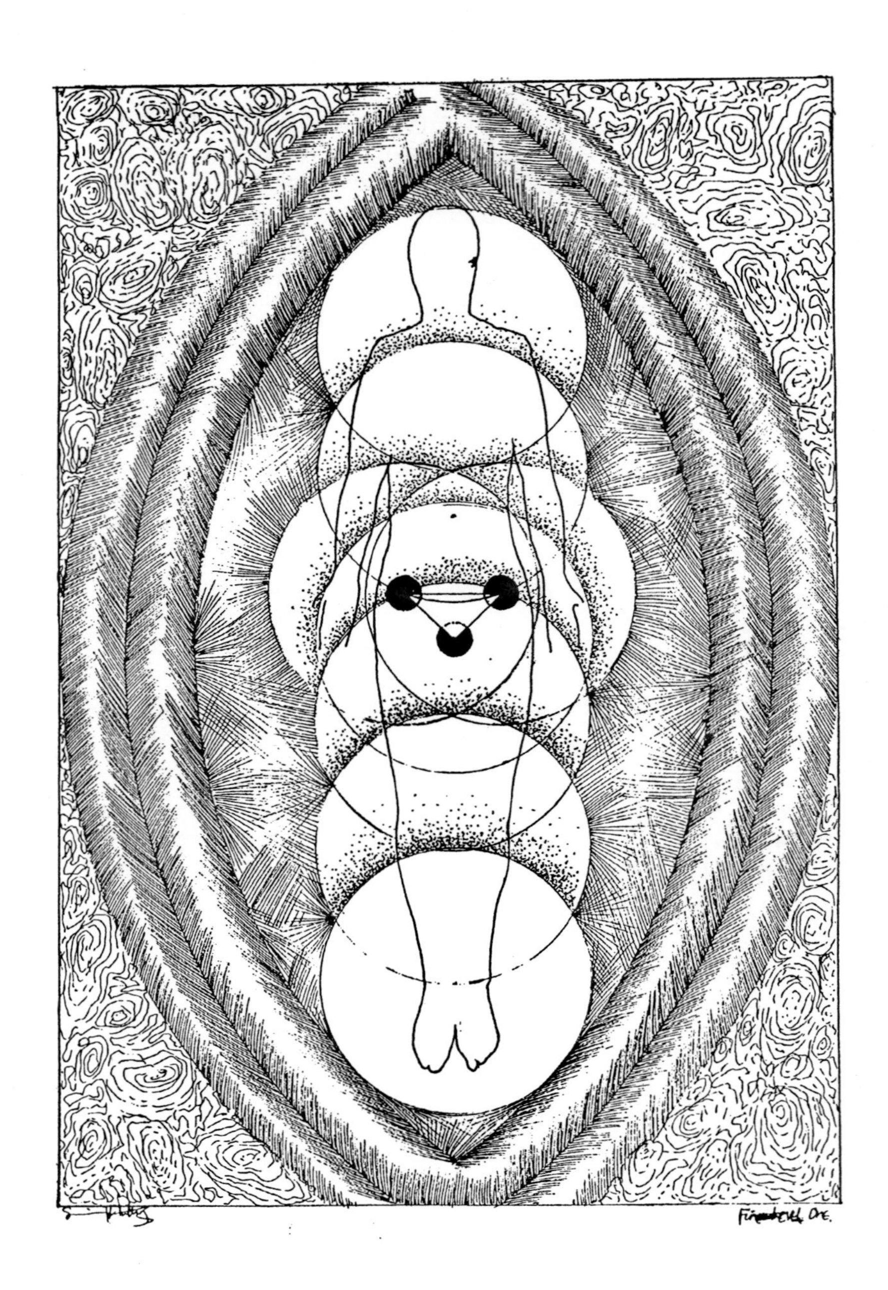

Fine level one

Fine level: one

What you need

Three smoky quartz crystals, an orange cloth. One crystal is placed point downwards on the pubic bone, the other two are placed slightly higher at the groin, where the legs meet the torso, with points outwards.

What this net can be used for

Added to another net to deepen the level of experience; helping the processes of healing and detoxification; a very deep contact with one's own centre and place of origin.

Although this is a very simple net it must be treated with great respect, for it is potentially extremely powerful. The stones are directly activating the base and second chakras and influence the body's centre-point, known as the hara, where our centre of gravity is located. Thus it is our most stable point, our centre and also our roots - the place from which we all must grow outwards.

If there is a need for detoxification this net can help to eliminate what is no longer required. If you know that there is a particular point in the body where toxins have accumulated, a herkimer diamond may be placed there to speed up the process. All detoxification means the removal of stored poisons and their passage through the body systems. With some toxins this can be extremely hazardous if not supervised correctly. At very least, it is vital to drink plenty of clean, pure water during the process to flush the toxins out of the body. Be aware that tiredness and headaches may follow as a result of the purification process.

A similar process is to place a sample of the substance to be removed in the centre point of the three crystals. This helps the body to recognise the foreign element in order to deal with it. It will be necessary with this procedure to check which other nets to use simultaneously or in sequence. Use dowsing or muscle-testing to determine the order and length of time needed.

In the same way as it tunes us into our own centre of gravity, this net also reaches out to other centres: the centre of the solar system, the galaxy, the universe, and can help us to recognise those distant and powerful forces of which we have little knowledge, but that shape the fundamental patterns of our reality.

Fine level: two

What you need

A dark pink cloth. One black tourmaline,placed on the central axis of the body, below the feet; two green tourmaline pointing inwards either side of the upper arm, level with the heart; one blue tourmaline on the central axis above the crown of the head; one pink tourmaline above the blue tourmaline on the same axis.

What this net can be used for

Integration of all subtle bodies, especially the finest; eases all planetary transits, particularly Saturn; access to different levels of consciousness and reality.

Tourmaline is one of the most useful crystals for balancing and restoring health. It has characteristic and unique electrical properties which means all varieties have a beneficial strengthening effect on the body's electromagnetic and electrical energies. Black tourmaline, often known as schorl, put below the feet protects from harmful environmental forces and also maintains a closer link to the Earth. Green tourmaline, verdelite, placed at the heart balances the emotional systems. Blue tourmaline, indicolite, above the crown helps to access fine levels of communication and transmits it into the mind for understanding. Pink tourmaline, a pale rubellite, further away from the top of the head, connects us to the flow of the universal energy of love allowing a free movement to anywhere in the universe.

As well as the energy fields of the physical body, the emotions and the mind, which surround and interpenetrate the physical body we have much finer energy bodies which are to do with

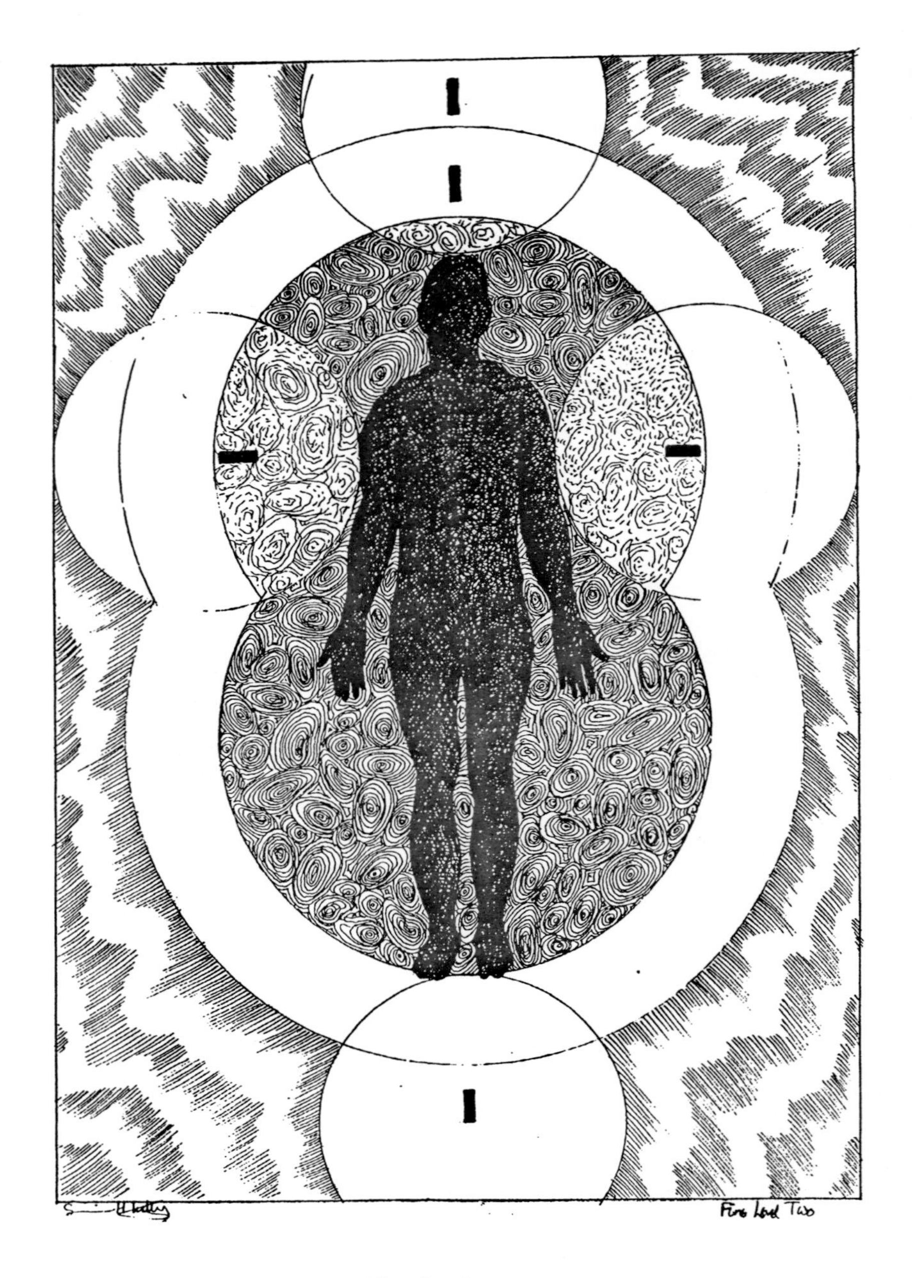

Fine level two

our more universal existence beyond normal time and space. These energy fields, sometimes called the soul body, causal body and spiritual body, do not fluctuate or change from day to day like the emotional and mental bodies but act more like supervisors and navigators steering us in the required directions in our lives to achieve our goals and learn lessons. They could be collectively labelled as the Higher Self, and are more aware of the ramifications and shifts of energy throughout existence. When all the subtle energy fields, or bodies, are integrated and working well together there is a correct flow of information and energy between them, neither too much nor too little, and this brings about a greater sense of wholeness and well-being.

All the subtle bodies are influenced by planetary positions - the tourmaline in this net help to align our energies so that we are the most comfortable we can be at times when awkward planetary juxtapositions are taking place.

Amethyst healing net

Amethyst healing net

What you need

Eight amethyst crystals, a yellow or violet cloth. The amethysts are placed at the top of the head and below the feet with the remaining six evenly spaced around the body. If the crystals have natural points these should be placed facing inwards. A tourmaline or smoky quartz may also be useful.

What this net can be used for

Any deep healing work; safe regressions; clarifying subtle perceptions; calming minds.

This net was the first to be used and has been in use for many years now. We have found that when some of the stones are larger than others, or when their energies are unequal, there may be a sensation of the body tipping backwards with head sinking or tipping forwards with feet sinking. These sensations are fairly common anyway in energy nets and are indicators of a re-adjustment of subtle energy. However, in this case it can usually be instantly corrected by matching stones with similar size or energy. If you have one amethyst larger than the rest it is usually best placed below the feet.

It is very easy to "drift away" in this net, and so when the session is coming to an end just carefully place a dark tourmaline crystal on the forehead. This will immediately bring the person back to the present. It has been described like being slammed back down on the table! Using a tourmaline or smoky quartz in this way can also be useful to bring calm if a healing crisis occurs.

Because amethyst works effectively with the mind and is linked with the subtle perceptions of the "third eye" between the eyebrows, those who are already somewhat psychically open or sensitive, may find they are spontaneously witnessing other-life events or new information. With the help of a trained therapist this net can be invaluable to access those areas of the past that need clearing away or resolving. If you wish to attempt this sort of work it is always advisable to have someone with you who knows the ins and outs of past life regression. The presence of so much amethyst helps to prevent unnecessary experiences or unwanted intrusions, but especially for inexperienced "travellers" there may be some feelings of fear or emotional upset which will need working through.

Another use for the amethyst healing net is to begin to learn to distinguish the energy effects of different gemstones and crystals. After a few minutes getting used to the net itself, once the body and mind have settled down, another person carefully places a stone on the forehead. This changes the energy pattern and can be experienced clearly by the experimenter. After a few minutes the stone is replaced by another, and so on. It helps to clarify the subjective experience if you can use stones roughly the same size and weight. Finish off with a grounding stone, like tourmaline, smoky quartz or haematite.

Attuning to whole entity energies

What you need

Five pieces of moldavite, four amethyst quartz, three clear quartz and a white cloth. You will need some tape to keep some stones in place. The moldavite is put in both hands and in the centre of the forehead. The remaining two pieces are taped on the top of the feet between the tendons of the first and second toes. Two pieces of clear quartz are placed either side of the body at about the level of the solar plexus, while the four amethysts are positioned either side of the legs just below the knees and above the head, one on each side at about shoulder width apart. The last clear quartz is positioned below the feet. If the amethyst and quartz are terminated, then the points should be directed inwards, towards the centre of the body.

What this net can be used for

Brings to the awareness the multi-dimensional and timeless nature of the Self; accessing information from the deepest levels of consciousness and different parts of the universe; alignment to Higher Self and true direction; self-integration, confidence and purpose.

Experience within this net will depend somewhat upon the belief systems of the individual, for example what symbols are important and how one understands time and space. This is a net where patience and openness are required. Very often information or energy is very subtle, or takes a form that is unexpected, such as appearing later in dreams, ideas or inspiration from "out of the blue". The experiences are often vague but should always feel satisfying and integrating.

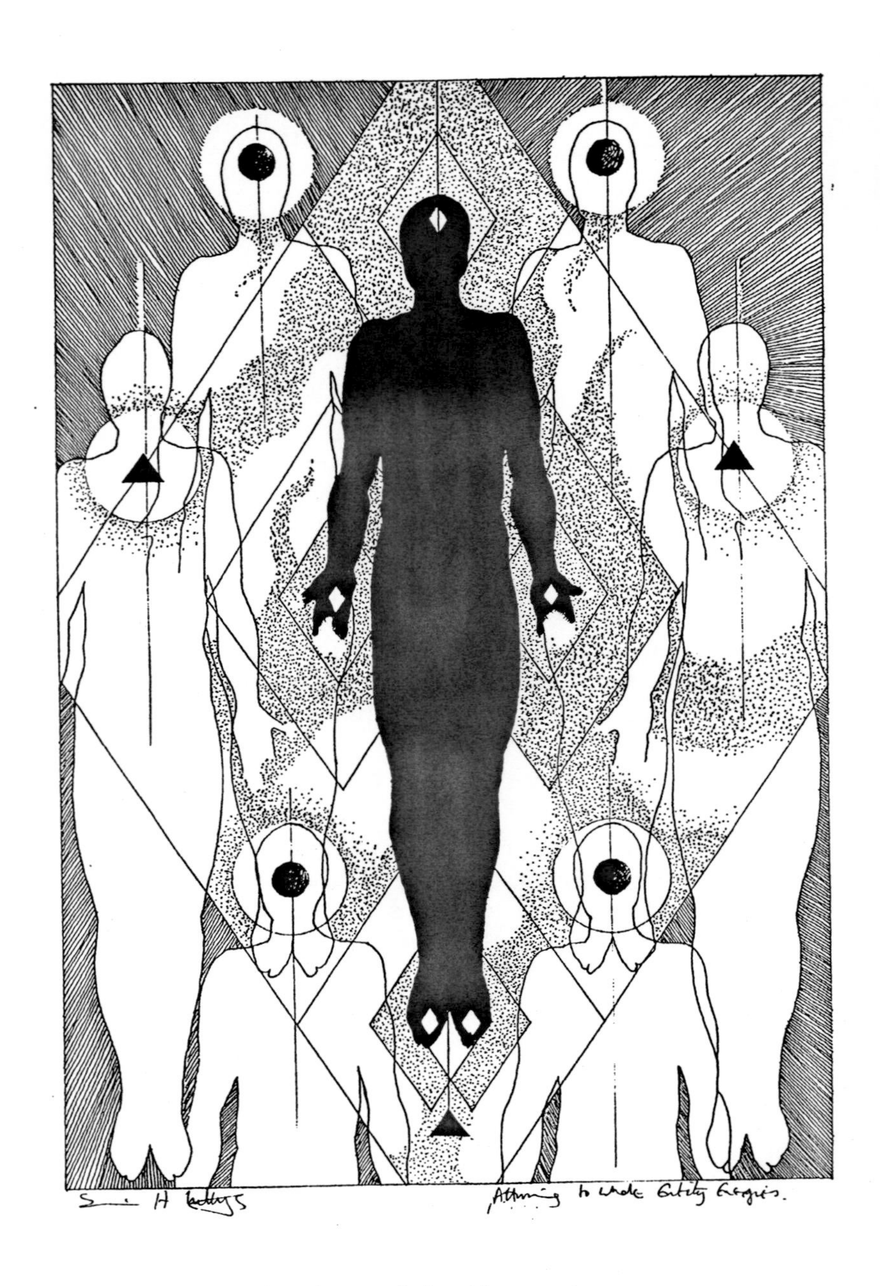

Attuning to whole entity energies

Moldavite is a powerful stone whose exact origin is not certain. Most people believe that it is either a fragmented comet or was created by the impact of a large comet on the earth's surface about fifteen million years ago. This translucent, bottle-green glassy stone comes only from a small area in Czechoslovakia, (although tektites of less brilliant colour are found in America, Java, Tibet and Australia), and forms a variety of shapes suggestive of its explosive molten origins. Experiences of moldavite do vary, but it certainly seems to activate latent abilities, speeds up healing processes and connects to the extra-planetary energies of the universe. In this net moldavite is the only stone that is in contact with the body, as if it were initiating a vibrational rate to speed up or refine the physical form, allowing it to contact finer realms of existence.

Amethyst is a major tool in healing and activates the functions of the Higher Self whilst creating a safe energy field in which to rest. Clear quartz helps to balance and strengthen the entire system, and here helps to balance particularly the third chakra to integrate new energy levels into the physical and acts as a doorway to other levels. The white cloth that is generally applicable can be replaced with a one representing the fundamental energy vibration, or core colour, of the person, if this is known.

If one looks at this net geometrically we have a pattern of 3:4:5: with an increasing vibratory pattern that is echoed in clear quartz:amethyst:moldavite. The downward pointing triangle of clear quartz anchoring and creating a flow into the physical; the amethyst rectangle establishing safe boundaries with the potential to expand, (whereas the equal sided square is static, the rectangle shows more dynamism); and the pentagon or pentagram of moldavite is the mediator between "above" and "below", the position and number of humankind.

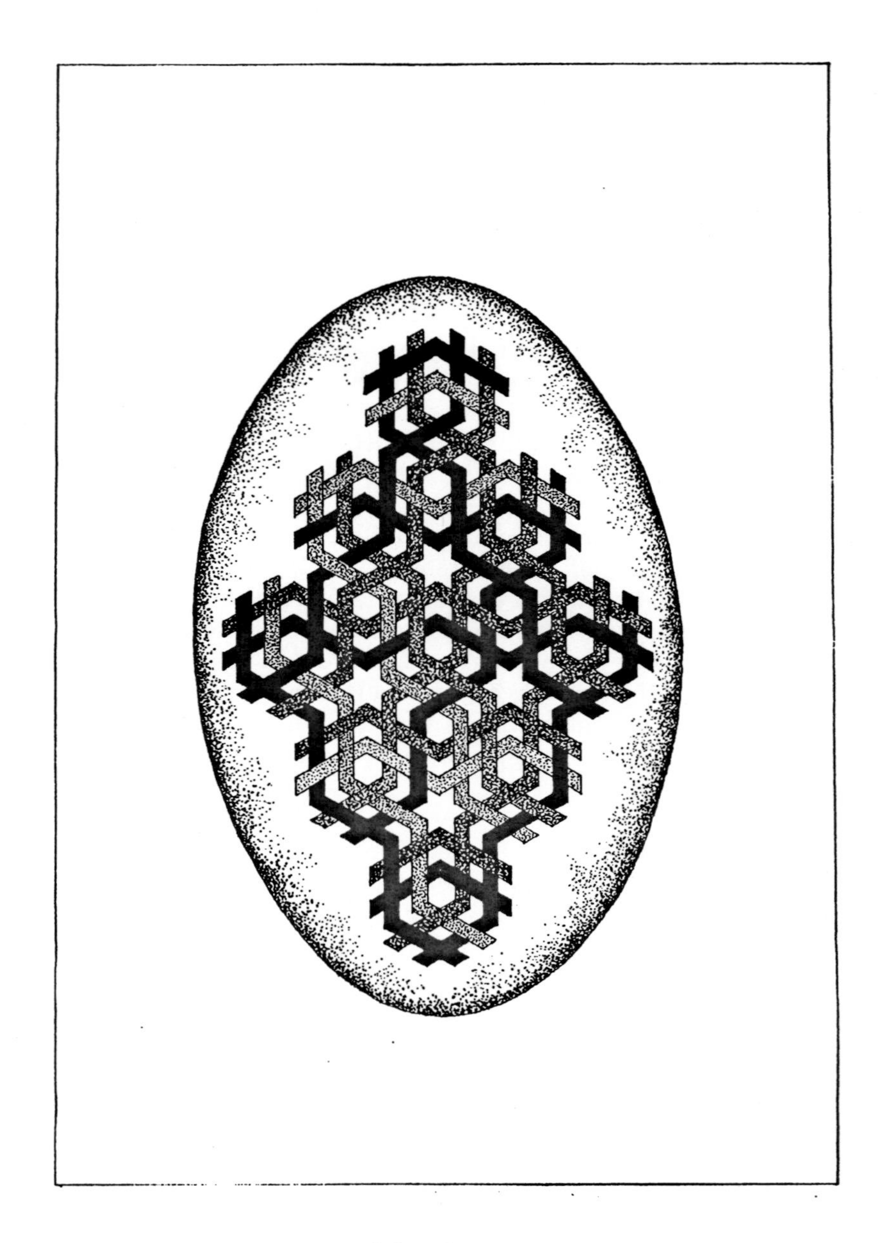

Colour key nets

Introduction to the colour-key nets

Light is the energy bath in which we have evolved. It is an ever-present nuance that colours our existence and as such it is very often taken for granted - like the pressure of the very air around us.

Life on the surface of the earth has evolved in the presence of light and has based its survival upon strategies for transforming and utilising light as its food. As humans we have developed eyes that recognise thousands of shades from the spectrum of visible light - far more precision than one would imagine could be of worthwhile survival value. Other mammals, for instance, have apparently less refined visual information, so why this efflorescence of visual acuity?

Whatever turns out to be the final answer, it can be assumed that there is a very good reason or Nature would not have invested so much energy in its development.

It is known, measurable and completely verified that change the colour of light and you will change the speed of chemical reaction. Some colours will increase the speed of reaction, other colours will decrease the speed. Now, as our bodies are an immeasurable welter of chemical reactions, it is no wonder that even at our most sensually obtuse/unaware we feel an emotional shift as we move from an environment of one predominant colour - say restaurant red to another, say of primrose yellow.

This is because colour is a real energy as much as electricity or magnetism. Colour is how our brains, via our eyes, interpret the energy tides of light that sweep our planet, mainly from the Sun, but also from distant stars.

Colour is of core importance to our being as it directly stimulates the hypothalamus deep within the brain, wrapped in the convolutions of the limbic system - the area thought to be responsible for deep emotions, memories triggered by smell, primal survival functions and the seat of the experience of pleasure.

Although the spectrum of light is a continuous band shifting from deep red to violet, human minds tend to distinguish seven main colours - the colours of the rainbow. Each of these colours is linked to activities and functions we have divided into physical, emotional, mental, spiritual and cosmic.

The names written alongside the colours are those we learned to associate with each colour during our training in colour therapy. It is a peculiar feature of the human mind that it tends to express energies in a way that is easily recognisable and often human in form. This gives us a point of contact and an ability to recognise and relate directly, it focuses on the particular and concrete rather than a nebulous abstraction.

The attributes and iconography of god-forms in any culture are a way to express and understand non-local, universally present and ever-present energies. They are also strong thought-forms through which that god/universal energy might wish to temporarily manifest in order to appear or to function in a more physical manner - to appear before its worshippers, perhaps.

The idea of "The Masters" was apparent in the Theosophical doctrines at the turn of the 20th century and elaborated in the writings of Alice Bailey. More recent writings rely quite substantially on her snippets of information and under closer examination don't seem to tell us an awful lot more. Alice Bailey's work is what would now be called "channelings" from a Master known to her as D.K. or Djwhal Khul, the Tibetan. In his dense and extensive dictations D.K. reveals a hierarchy of spiritually developed souls, some embodied, some on "higher planes" who guide and teach the awakening humanity. It's a bit like a spiritual Open University with tutors of various skills guiding the initiate through paths of discovery in specific subject areas. Those areas have professors who are the Ascended Masters themselves, directing the work of world evolution in their chosen specialities. The concept of hidden Wisdom Schools is nothing new, yet this particular model, expressed in terms of pre-War social experience can make many people feel nervous and uncomfortable. Nor is this much helped by spacey-brained "New-Agers" who will channel any Ascended Master you choose faster than you can say "unconditional drivel".

Our own experience with these Master Energies as we have explored them through the Colour Key Energy Nets, neither accepts or rejects the nuts and bolts of Alice Bailey's system, but perhaps broadens out the concepts to make them more generally workable to those familiar with other philosophical systems.

Firstly, we see Masters, not as superhuman social workers, but as localised expressions of a certain type of universal energy that is a real part of each of us as much as every other being, sentient or non-sentient. The apparent individuality of personality, sense of humour, and predilection for certain types of information or knowledge that we might recognise as say, Lao Tsu or Kuthumi is merely a useful lens to focus the universal abstract down to the earthly particular. Whether the actual historical or mythical form is "real" in itself, the Master Energy can focus through that form because of the type of being and the type of characteristics it exhibited.

Or to put it another way - within the universal energies we know locally in this solar system as colour - every individual being will, at any one time, be functioning within a range of one or more of those energies. If that being spends a large part of its life aligned to one aspect it may become a vehicle for that energy beyond the physical life.

Those of you who wish to explore the Colour Key Nets with all this in mind may discover you are already familiar with some of the energy signatures. You may recognise the presence of gods and goddesses you have worked with in ritual and meditation, and if you work with more than one system you may be already aware that a particular god-form in one tradition has an exact energy-feel to a god-form in another tradition.

What we are suggesting here is that you don't get hung up with names or other superficial identifying tags whether they be Neteru, Ascended Masters, Bodhisattvas or Aessir. Explore as many facets of each lens as you wish and in the end you may realise what any Tibetan Tantrika will eventually discover - the god that arises and dances in front of you is none other than an aspect of your own Self and ultimately there is nothing else other than That.

Footnote

As the authors consider that each "Master" energy is an aspect of Universal Awareness from which all beings are constituted, it follows that everyone has the ability to tune into or channel any one of these energies. We have no quarrel with this, merely with the quality of the interpretation of energy into language which so often falls on the sloppy side of sentimentality or the aggravating side of banality - let alone the patronising tone!

Red - The Christ net

What you need

A white cloth, twelve clear quartz crystals and one ruby. The quartz crystals are placed points outwards around the body. Start with one above the head, then one below the feet and evenly space the others five to a side. The ruby is placed over the heart. Small ruby crystals or slices of ruby are quite easy to find and shouldn't cost very much - certainly a lot less that gem quality stones!

What this net can be used for

Attuning to the colour red and The Christ Master Energy; energy to achieve one's desires; getting to grips with reality; opening up, being oneself; protection; empowerment; relinquishing guilt.

Red is the energy of gravity - it pulls things together and activates. Its core emotion is the desire to be, and so in all forms of manifestation and creation this energy is always the first to emerge. It is the energy of matter, of being, and relates to our existence in the world and also to the Earth itself. It is fundamental, literally, to all practicalities in everyday life. Red is the grasp of and ability to work with reality. Red is the clay from which God made the first being, Adam ("red-man").

Red is the blood that courses through us and the passion for life that should be ours every second of our existence. The loss of red, or of blood, is a sign of danger - a sign that our very survival is at risk. Using and maintaining our own red energy, in all its aspects, is our only protection from harm.

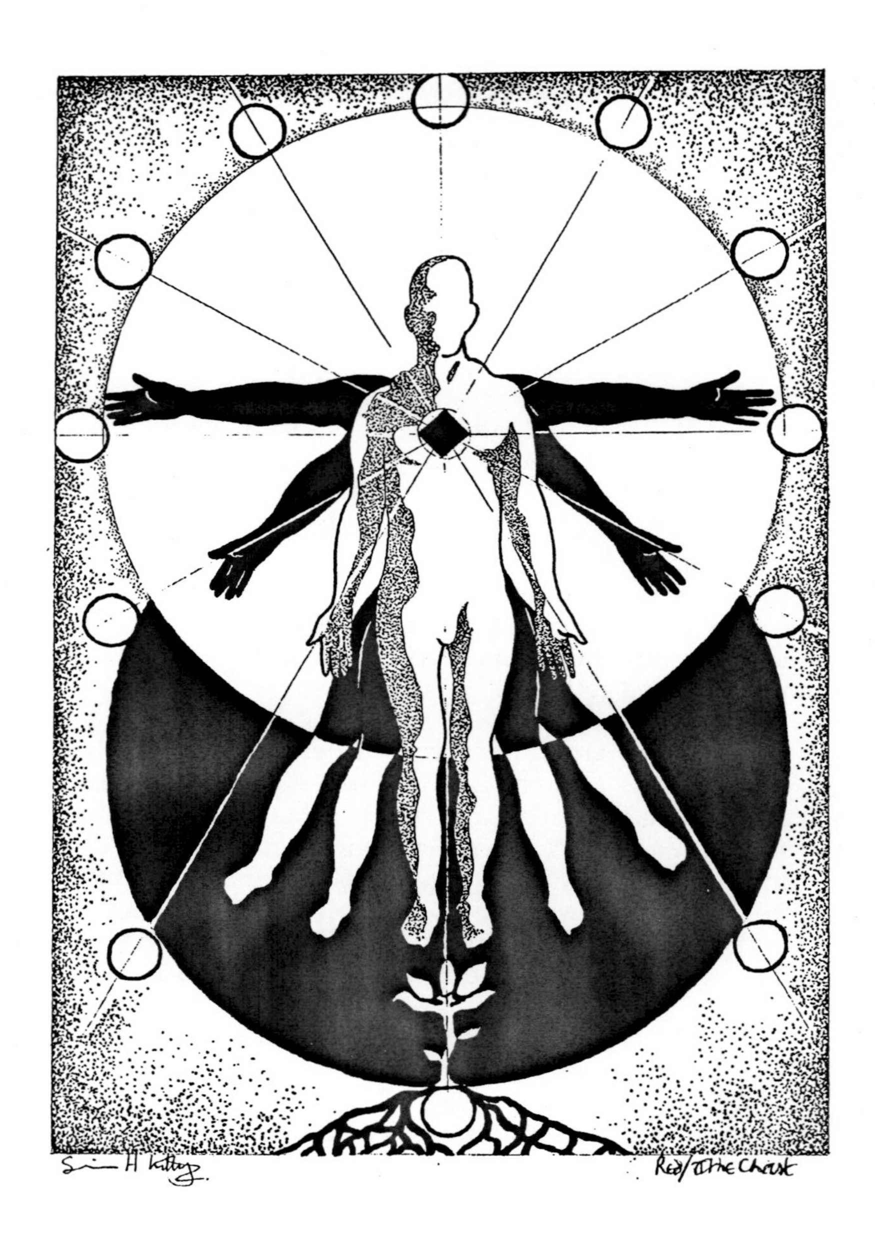

Red - The Christ

In its essence then, red is the passion to be, it is practicality, the ability to survive and prosper in the world, protection from harm, union and support within Earth's energies, energy and zest.

As red is the first energy to manifest in creation and is the most physical aspect of Spirit, so The Christ appears as the Spirit made flesh and blood. As a symbol, the Christ reminds us (and of this we need constant reminding!), that physicality and physical existence is as holy as any other state of being.

Red is not a patient energy. Red is the Now energy. If we were to allow ourselves to live in the fullness and holiness of the Present we would not only have the limitless energy of the universe at our disposal, but we would be manifesting the energy of the Cosmic Christ. Unfortunately, the political development of Christianity favoured the promulgation of passive peace, waiting for salvation and suffering in silence until that time when it makes no political or social difference that someone has found freedom (ie. after death). This was in no way the teaching of the aspect of Christ, who historically and mythologically appeared as Jesus Christ. There was nothing "meek and mild" about Jesus - his role was pure red energy, motivating, energising, empowering and following the path of active peace. The peaceful warrior.

The Master energy known as The Christ contains within it the energy of the historical person, but extends far beyond all human boundaries of history, place, persuasion and so on. In many belief systems the firstborn of the Creator will manifest the Red Christ Master energy, because the eldest child, the firstborn, is the first act of creation, the first transmutation of the material of God into tangible, physical form.

Ruby at the heart activates the core energy of the individual, as well as the physical well-being of the heart and circulatory system. The heart is the centre of our being, where we feel from, where we can be hurt most, and from where courage springs to act and to be. One has only to list the phrases and imagery related to the heart to recognise how central a concept it is.

Quartz crystals surrounding the body with points outwards help to release pent-up energies focused on the heart, cleansing the sense-of-worth of false or imposed guilt and sin. They also allow the creative energies a pathway out into the world, to connect with the goals for which we reach. The symbolic significance of twelve in this net is obvious and manyfold, from disciples (the means to spread one's energy into the world), to astrological signs (the archetypal energies of existence).

Do not expect this net to be gentle and soft, but rather like a gust of wind blowing away cobwebs and sending a shiver of expectant coolness down your spine. Although The Christ Master Energy is powerful, it still comes from the heart of creation and so is filled with a strong compassion for all beings and all suffering.

Orange - Lao Tsu and Kwan Yin net

What you need

An orange cloth and twelve crystals of smoky quartz. The quartz is evenly spaced around the body with points outwards.

What this net can be used for

Attuning to the Master Energies of healing and compassion; deeply cleansing and purifying; deep healing on all levels; removal of toxicities; increase of wisdom, humour and creativity.

Orange is the energy of red added to the energy of yellow. Red by itself is energising and motivating but often hasn't a clue about directing itself. It just wants to get on and do it. Orange energy takes the power of red and channels it in those directions where it is needed most. Red is the power of a burst dam, orange is the channel through which that force of water can be directed for the benefit of all. Hence orange is a universally powerful healing vibration. Any situation where there is a block to the proper flow of life, such as in the case of injury, shock or trauma, whether life-threatening or momentary, orange quickly restores the flow to its proper channels and brings about the conditions for healing. Orange is so creative for the same reasons - it can remove blocks in the way of growth - and creativity, in all its aspects, is the expression of Life to continually expand, experiencing more and more.

In all cases of healing, on whatever level, once the energy blocks are removed they must be flushed away so they do not have a chance to reform somewhere else. As we have

Orange - Lao Tsu and Kwan Yin

mentioned elsewhere, all detoxification processes are more comfortable to go through when given a helping hand. Drinking regular small amounts of spring water is very useful, as is keeping the diet light and balanced. Using the Orange Master Net for short periods on a regular basis will also help to clear the energy systems of released debris and speed up the healing process.

We know this Master energy by the names of Kwan Yin and Lao Tsu. Kwan Yin is the Chinese goddess of compassion and mercy. In the Kwan Yin Sutra it says of her: "*Whoever hears her name, whoever sees her and remembers her unceasingly, will extinguish the sorrows of existence...*", and again she is "*the numinous cloud of compassion pouring forth spiritual rain like sweet nectar to quench the flames of agony....whose compassionate eye beholds all beings, a boundless ocean of blessings..*". Kwan Yin is said to have made the following pledge "*....forever and everywhere will I live and strive for the redemption of every creature throughout the world from the bonds of conditioned existence*".

In the West this compassionate energy is often equated with Mary, The Mother of God, who intercedes with God and His Son on behalf of mankind for the forgiveness of sins and the removal of suffering.

Lao Tsu, the historical, but also legendary, founder of Taoism, is the male expression of the orange Master energy. He lived in the 6th century BC at the same time as Confucius (Kung Fu Tsu), and whereas the latter formulated rules for proper conduct and behaviour, Lao Tsu taught the mysteries of the Spirit. At the end of his life Lao Tsu was persuaded to write down his philosophy. This became known as the famous *Tao Te Ching, the Book of Virtue in the Way*. The Tao, often translated as *The Way* or *Natural Law*, is ultimately about flowing with Life rather than struggling against it. By observing the patterns of the world and by acknowledging the equality of all beings, everything can be achieved. Ultimately Taoism is about invisibility - blending so well with the Universe that we make no ripples and so cease from suffering.

" *The Universe is sacred.*
You cannot improve it.
If you try to change it, you will ruin it.
If you try to hold it, you will lose it".

(Chapter 29)

"..*The sage takes care of all men and abandons no one.*
He takes care of all things and abandons nothing."
"(Chapter 27)

"..*In dwelling, be close to the land.*
In meditation, go deep in the heart.
In dealing with others, be gentle and kind.
In speech, be true.
In ruling, be just.
In business, be competent.
In action, watch the timing.
No fight: No blame.

(Chapter 8)

"..*Stand before it and there is no beginning.*
Follow it and there is no end.
Stay with the ancient Tao,
Move with the present.

Knowing the ancient beginning is the essence of Tao".
(Chapter 8)

(Translations by Gia Fu Feng)

When we encounter the Master Energy of Lao Tsu, it is gentle and wise with a huge sense of humour, full of pun and paradox. The wisdom of Orange is in allowing things to flow to their proper place, rather than trying to understand and label, and thereby limit, everything. In this way there is nothing that cannot be put right, nothing that cannot be healed.

Gold - Sanat Kumara

What you need

Twelve clear quartz, one citrine and a yellow cloth. The quartz crystals are laid evenly spaced around the body with points inwards. The citrine quartz is placed above the clear quartz at the top of the head with its point down towards the body.

What this net can be used for

Attunement to the creative organising forces of this solar system; loving intelligence; clarity and harmony with one's purpose; wisdom from the Higher Self: decision making based on wisdom; enhancing all functions of the mind.

The colour to have in mind here is not a metallic gold but a very rich yellow - yellow with still a hint of orange, a saffron yellow. This colour is primarily to do with assimilation and organisation on every level. It is the colour of our sun and is thus very close to the creative motivation of our solar system.

In the *Brahmana Purana*, Sanat Kumara is the cause of the ninth in a sequence of creations:

> "*The ninth creation called the Kaumara, that is brought about by Kumara*". (1.1.5, 78)

the text goes on:

> "*Kratu and Sanatkumara, these two lived in perpetual celibacy. They were born before, they are the elders to all.... They shine refulgently in the world by means of the splendour of their own souls. Both of them were yogins by nature. These two, of great power, carried out the duties*

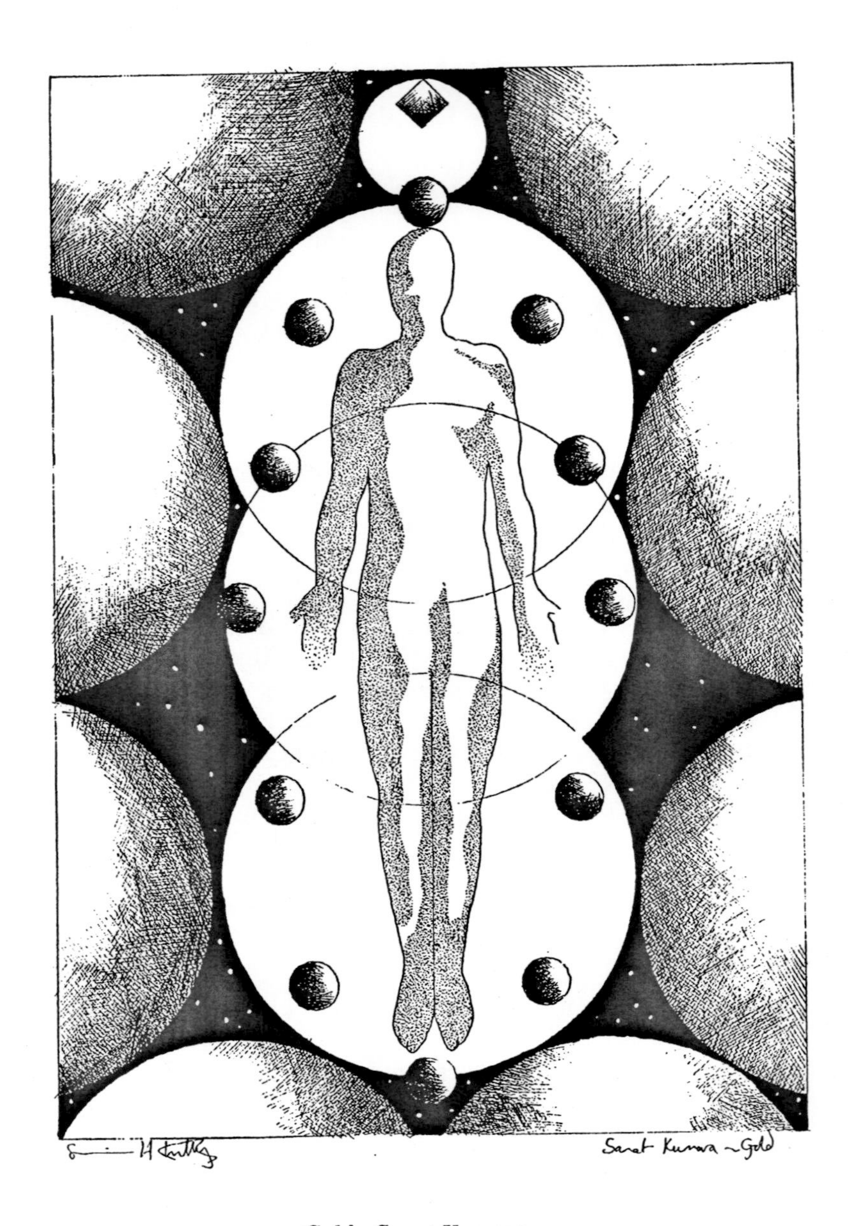

Gold - Sanat Kumara

of subjects and love by superimposing the soul on the supreme soul by means of the soul. He continues to be in the same state as he was in, when he was born. So he is called Kumara. Thereupon his name Sanat Kumara became well established. "(1.1.5, 79-82)

"*sanat kumara*" can be translated as eternal youth, or eternal son. As an entity or an energy he remains celibate, that is, he doesn't personally become involved in further creation. It is for this reason the Creator Brahma has to create mind-born sons from various parts of his body in order to continue the development of the Universe, and this is why Sanat Kumara is said to be the cause of the ninth phase of creation. Sanat Kumara is a yogin, that is, perfectly established in Unity, existing within his own Self, remaining above the creation, not becoming involved yet still carrying out important functions "superimposing the soul on the supreme soul".

Each of the Master Energies within the colour yellow emphasise certain aspects of that vibration. From these, albeit obscure, references, Sanat Kumara can be thought of as a focussing of the knowledge and wisdom of the Higher Self in a manner where it remains forever unchanged yet overseeing and empowering the rest of creation with its own splendour and love.

In another way Sanat Kumara is the energy that allows the mechanics of creation to continue in an orderly, organised fashion, by being the cauldron that holds creation's ingredients seething away inside its stable form.

As Alice Bailey writes in "*Rays and Initiations*" (p. 371);

" *Sanat Kumara...is the coherent force within the planet, holding through His Radiatory influence all forms and all substances in the planetary form so that they constitute one coherent, energised and functioning whole...The basic purpose of Sanat Kumara is to bring about the right relations in every field of his manifested life*".

The Gold - Sanat Kumara Net aligns us to those aspects of the yellow light vibration that bring us to self-knowledge and a state of wisdom characteristic of the functioning of the Higher Mind, where there is perfect clarity of what we are, what we are not; when to act and when to remain still; what information is of use and what is to be discarded, and so on.

Yellow - Lady Portia

What you need

Seven pieces of lapis lazuli, five clear quartz tumbled stones and a blue cloth. Lapis lazuli is placed above the head; quartz level with the ears on both sides; lapis on either side of the shoulders; quartz on both sides level with the diaphragm and solar plexus area; lapis beside the hands and to the side of the feet; quartz below the feet on the central axis.

What this net can be used for

Mental clarity; judgement; discernment and the balancing of polarities; reestablishing balance at all levels - physical, emotional, mental, spiritual; helps access the truth of any situation; discrimination; helps disclose your own truth - your destiny.

This net attunes to the quality of the yellow vibration that activates and accelerates the functioning of the clear-thinking mind and the discriminating intelligence of judgement. As we have said, yellow is primarily an energy of assimilation and organisation. In this aspect, known to us as Portia, and also Maat, these energies are used to bring all relevant available information to the conscious awareness, so that they can be organised, labelled and categorised. Once this is achieved, and only then, a true and correct judgement of any situation can be given. Portia deals with the big issues of Truth and Justice and how they are used or misused on all levels of creation.

Now, what may appear to be true on one level of reality is not necessarily true for another level. For example, in dream reality you may be living on a desert island, but to someone else in waking reality you will be fast asleep in your bed.

Yellow - Lady Portia

Neither one perception is wrong, yet neither is fully correct. It is the assumption that one person is right and another wrong, that one thing is true and another not true, that leads to the continuation of injustice and suffering in the world. This situation arises from the imbalanced use of other yellow energies. Sense of personal integrity and power, one's own memory and personal interpretation of sense data helps to create one's own identity, that is, the apparent boundaries of what is and is not us. This self-created being, strong in itself, we call the ego.Now although the ego wields considerable power it always has a sneaking suspicion that something, some information, or some blindingly obvious fact, has been left out of the carefully constructed equation of what it is. However, so much energy has been invested in building up and maintaining a satisfactory picture of reality that the ego is extremely unwilling to accept it may be wrong in some of its deductions. In order to maintain its unrivalled position, the ego personality begins to play power games to assert its own view of reality on others.

The energy of Lady Portia exists at a level of true understanding where all viewpoints and all experiences are taken into account. Nothing is overlooked, nothing is disguised. It is the level of knowledge and speech known in Sanskrit as "*ritam*" - absolute Truth where no falsehood or illusion can exist.

In ancient Egypt the pharaohs ruled by virtue of Maat. If they upheld universal Law and Truth they were legitimised in the eyes of the gods and worthy to rule the land and its people. Maat's symbol was the feather and it was this feather that was placed opposite the soul of the deceased on the Scales of Judgement after death.

Should the soul weigh heavier than Maat's feather it would be unable to travel to the paradise of the stars, where the gods dwelt, until its sins had all been cleansed away. The Balance was held by Tehuti (Thoth), the messenger and teacher of the gods, who represents yet another aspect of the yellow vibration - clarity, intelligence, learning and memory.

Lapis lazuli has been regarded as a royal stone for millennia. It is ideal in this net as one of its primary functions is to stimulate the deeper faculties of the mind, expand awareness and clarity, remove blocks from the memory and access a more universal wisdom. Some find lapis lazuli a little too intense for comfort and so the addition of tumbled quartz to the net allows a gentle, omnidirectional cleansing and smoothing out of released blocks and areas of turbulence. Using a blue cloth brings in the energy of communication and flow, making a connection to universal levels from which true information can be gathered without impediment.

Pale yellow - Kuthumi

What you need

Six clear quartz crystals and a yellow cloth. All crystals are placed with their points upwards, towards the north. One crystal is placed above the crown of the head; one on each side at the shoulders; one on the solar plexus, (this is the only crystal on the body); one on the outside of each foot.

What this net can be used for

Release of fears and anxiety; increase of joy; expansion of self; harmony and blissfulness with surroundings; free flow of information; communion with life; protection from power-draining situations; attunement to animal kingdoms.

This aspect of the yellow vibration is more earthly and softer than the others. It can be seen as the bright, pale yellow of a sunny day when everything is relaxed and content in the world. The Kuthumi energy, also found in the Theosophical texts as Master KH, or Koot Hoomi, is probably best recognised by us in the historical figure of St. Francis of Assisi. St. Francis created the least belligerent, least political and most peace-loving, (and most sane), of all the Christian Orders - the Franciscans. Francis's attunement to and compassion for all beings, expressed in his life and prayers, parallels that of Gautama Buddha. Indeed, the Buddha-to-come, known as Maitreya, is said to manifest the same Kuthumi energy.

The pale yellow - Kuthumi energy is all about contentment and joy, and most of all, complete lack of fear. Fear is the biggest problem there is. Were fears to be eliminated, all false barriers would disappear and a true communication on the level of the heart would occur. We would be free from the need

Pale yellow - Kuthumi

to capture other's power because we would be established in our own; we would be free from false boundaries and the distinctions of superiority and inferiority, right and wrong, matter and spirit; and, like St. Francis, having no fear to radiate into the environment, we would be able to co-exist and understand perfectly all other beings who share this world with us. The true Buddha-nature would emerge.

This net helps to remove tension and fear from the solar plexus, while at the same time anchoring us in the positive power of our true Self, which focuses in this area of the body. The surrounding pentagram of clear quartz stones reaffirms our link with the physical world and the power of our humanity. It brings the understanding and realisation that we shape the world with our minds and our beliefs, and that we can choose whether we are here to laugh and enjoy or to fear and suffer.

Pale green - Hilarion

Pale green - Hilarion

What you need

A black cloth, seven pieces of moldavite and six tourmalines of various colours, at least one of which is green. If moldavite is not available it can be replaced with any type of tourmaline. A green tourmaline is placed on the heart area, all other stones are around the body. Tourmaline is placed both sides of the torso level with the solar plexus/diaphragm. Moldavite is on either side of the shoulders and a tourmaline is above the crown of the head. Moldavite is positioned just below the hands, at about mid-thigh level, and tourmaline beside each foot. On the central axis of the body between the feet, but below the level of the tourmalines, put a moldavite. The two remaining moldavites are placed at the same level as the tourmalines above the head, but they are positioned so that they are further out from the body than all the rest of the stones. As you can see, the tourmalines and moldavites are placed alternately.

What this net can be used for

Re-establishing personal space; sense of freedom; discovering one's true direction and path in any situation; clarification of spiritual path; attunement to the Earth and its life, especially the plant kingdoms; calmness.

There are two nets that reflect the vibration of green, each emphasising different aspects. Green is the colour of harmonious balance. It comes midway along the visible light spectrum, and is also associated with the heart chakra, the balance point in the body's physical and spiritual makeup. The whole of the chest area - heart, lungs and arms - is often characterised in everyday language by expressions that show our understanding of its effects. "My hands were tied" - indicating lack of personal choice; "My heart wasn't in it" - a lack of enthusiasm or powerlessness; "I just couldn't breathe" - sense of oppression or suppressed personal choice; "a weight on my shoulders" - sense of responsibility; "green" - as in young, inexperienced, naive; "green with envy" - seeing a desirable goal but unable to reach it.

The green vibration is thus associated with personal space and a sense of freedom and the ability, or lack of ability, to express oneself "from the heart". The other common association with green is, of course, the plant kingdom, and by extension, the world of Nature and the planet itself. In other words, the exterior, objective means by which we can experience our freedom by "going out into the world". Green is all about expansion, growth and power. It is able to grow and increase power by its faculty of balancing extremes such as expansion and contraction, (as in the lungs and heart), creation and destruction (as in all growth processes where the old form must vanish for the new to take its place), freedom and discipline, (freedom finding a new path, discipline in not straying from it).

The purpose of all growth and change is power. Power is the ability to control more and more of one's environment in a way that is supportive of more growth and the attaining of more power and so on. The motivation and cause of all growth, and all evolution is to increase power - to expand, to fill all available space, to become every thing, to extend one's boundaries endlessly. As the motivation of all existence, power is not "bad", nor should it be considered as morally dangerous. Indeed, it is the right of every being to be full of power. The only human problem with power is that it is not evenly distributed. Rather than choosing to grow truly powerful themselves, some people choose to prevent others from growing, thereby maintaining a sense of control by stealing or manipulating others' power. In the short term this leads to mass frustration, "heart-ache" and lack of fulfilment. In the long term the nature of green will manifest an explosion of growth and change as rebellions or revolutions in those societies who repress the creative desires of its members.

It is said that knowledge is power, or rather more accurately, the use of knowledge is power. The power of knowing about a subject area gives one more power to make use of that area. Among the masses of material channelled over the last few decades (which before the use of that term would probably have been called "inspired"!), some of the more interesting have been received from the Hilarion energy. This information covers such subjects as the properties of plants and herbs, vibrational remedies, and use of names and symbols. Hilarion is the energy exploring all aspects of the natural world. It is curiosity and the joy of discovery that increases our understanding and harmony within life.

Dark green - Djwhal Khul

Dark green - Djwhal Khul

What you need

Twelve pieces of moldavite are evenly spaced around the body with one above the head and one below the feet. The cloth is black.

What this net can be used for

Re-discovering and re-applying forgotten knowledge; understanding the more distant parts of creation - other galaxies, stars and so on; clarifies astrological information; helps with understanding the works of Alice Bailey; for innovators, outsiders, heretics and aliens.

The colour dark green is associated with the more universal or cosmic aspects of knowledge. The Master Energy is known as Djwhal Khul, DK, or The Tibetan who was the source behind all Alice Bailey's work and who is said to have dictated "*The Secret Doctrine*" to H. Blavatsky. In his own words:

"*On November 19th 1919, I made my first contact with A.A.B. (much to her distress and dismay), and I have worked steadily with her ever since.*"

He is perceived as an elderly Tibetan who works with healers and those who research into new ways of bringing harmony to the Earth. Understanding is perhaps the key word of DK's function. As he himself states at the beginning of "Initiation Human and Solar":

"*I am one who has wrestled and fought his way to a greater measure of light....and I must therefore act as a transmitter of the light....My work is to teach and spread the knowledge of the*

Ageless Wisdom wherever I can find a response, and I have been doing this for many years....The books that I have written are sent out with no claim for their acceptance. They may, or may not, be correct, true and useful. It is for you to ascertain their truth by right practice and by the exercise of intuition..." (August 1934).

Here is the stance of one who works within the energy of dark green, whoever they may be. Very often such people are perceived as rebels, heretics and madmen. They are bringing forward ideas. They do not even say "This is a new reality, believe it", but put forward concepts, hypotheses and "what if's". Even so, the guardians against innovation, those august institutions of established fact, turn against them because a false status quo is being challenged. Virtually all worthwhile inventions and all huge leaps forward in understanding have been accomplished by loners and "outsiders". Usually there is official inertia and resistance to change but in time - and it can be a long time indeed - change percolates through to the mass of humanity and eventually comes up as a loud "Why not?".

Freedom of speech, freedom of intellect, freedom of thought and imagination - the organic growth of synthesis and creativity - whenever and wherever allowed, brings a cultural and spiritual "renaissance" of benefit to all. The energy of DK is the non-violent Revolution of the Mind moving towards dynamic and evolutionary growth. It is the courage to be different and to pioneer unknown territory, "to boldly go where no-one has gone before".

Turquoise - Maha Chohan

What you need

Three celestite, three moldavites and a green cloth. The stones are placed alternately: celestite is at the crown, moldavite either side at shoulder level, celestite by the hands and a moldavite centrally placed beneath the feet.

What this net can be used for

Helping to establish one's means of soul expression; knowing how to express who and what you truly are; individuality; innovation; maintaining and strengthening the immune system; attuning to the Master Energies of Maha Chohan.

Turquoise is a melding of the energies of blue and green, so uniting the characteristics of each. In its essence it can be summed up as "the flow of the heart" or "communication of balance". It is the integration of growth with the outflowing of expression and as such is very life-enhancing and life-supporting. Turquoise is the full revealing of the unique self as a natural unselfconscious outpouring of life. Its physical correlate is the thymus gland located between heart and throat under the sternum. Until recently the thymus was thought only to be active during childhood growth but it is now known to play a vital part in maintaining the body's immunity against disease. On subtle levels the thymus is a major source of personal life-force and energy - the need to be fully oneself, a unique individual, distinct yet integrated with the universe. The food the soul requires is to be free to communicate its uniqueness. Whenever this food is denied, by the self or by others, energy drains from the system, failure and distress increase and the physical ability to resist disease diminishes.

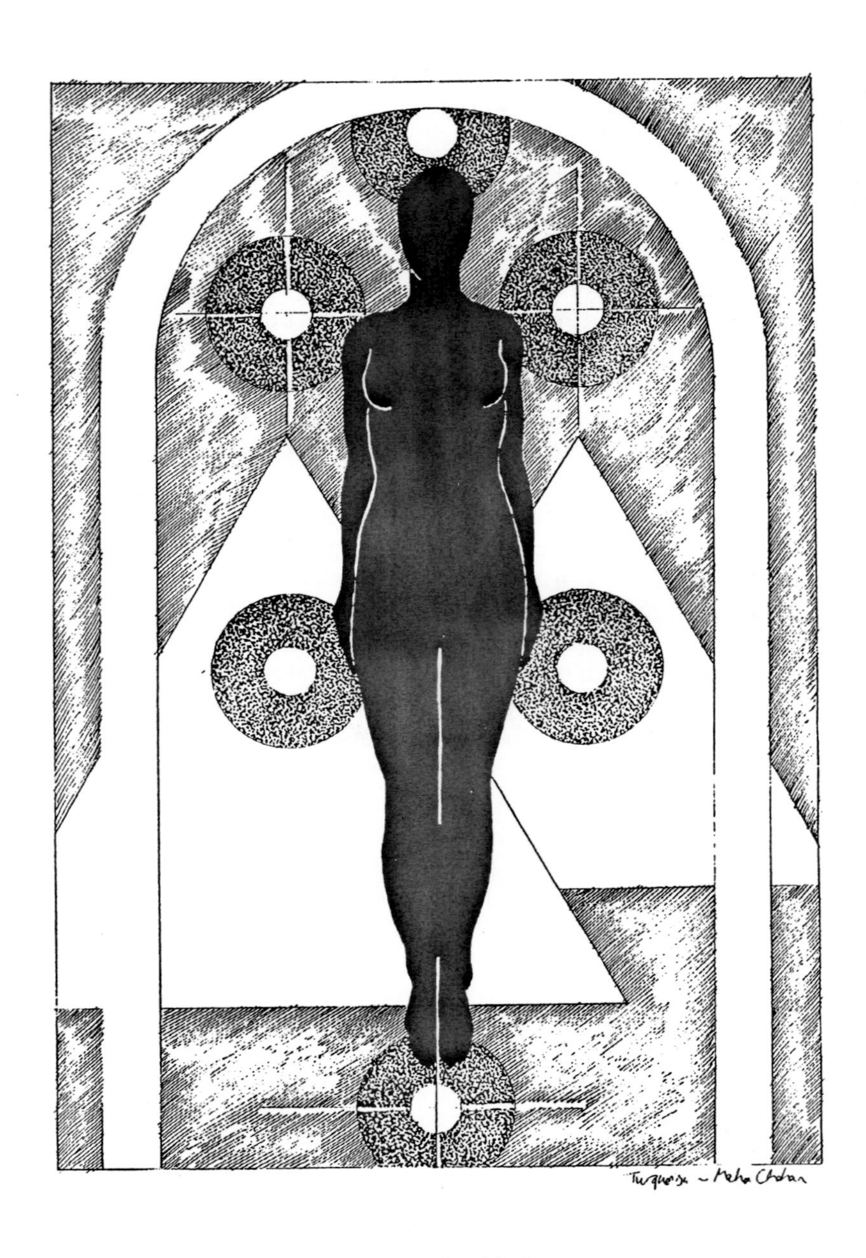

Turquoise - Maha Chohan

Turquoise is the vibration of interpretation. Information is integrated into the heart (the centre, the core), and expressed in a novel way appropriate to individual experience. Learning "parrot-fashion" is a blue activity, learning "by heart" is turquoise. Because of this characteristic turquoise comes into play wherever re-assessment and re-creation exist. Rediscovery of old ideas, new uses for everyday items or experiences, recycling on every level, is what turquoise is about.

The Master Key associated with turquoise is known to us as Maha Chohan, the Master of Civilisation, one of the three superconscious entities, according to Alice Bailey. Maha Chohan represents "the sumtotal of the intelligence aspect", which expresses through active intelligence, personal independence, leadership qualities, adaptability and creative communication. The role of Maha Chohan Bailey defines as the:

"..*fostering and strengthening of that relation between spirit and matter, life and form, the self and the not-self, which results in what we call civilisation*". (Initiation, Solar and Human).

As such, the role of this energy pattern fosters science, education and the processes of civilisation, which is adaptive learning: the integration and synthesis of groups of people towards a common set of ideals, and which, in its truest form, is synergistic rather than exclusive.

Moldavite is one of THE growth stones. It tends to amplify all life-enhancing qualities and gives an energy boost to the activity of other stones used alongside it. As it has connections to outer space moldavite helps us to see ourselves from a larger perspective - and the larger the perceptual flowerpot we find ourselves in, the better our roots are for absorbing the basic nutrient of growth, that is, ideas. As a stone that balances our energies through the heart chakra too, moldavite will stimulate the desire to grow out from ourselves and celestite gives us a fine, celestial voice with which to accomplish our goals.

If you feel stuck in a mould and wish to break out, use this net. If they broke the mould when you were made and you feel uncomfortable with your uniqueness, this net will clarify and bring insight. If you are grappling with difficult concepts or are attempting to revive half-forgotten knowledge, or if you are on the edge of scientific credibility, yet feel a breakthrough of understanding is imminent, use the Turquoise Net to crystallise your thoughts.

Blue - El Morya

What you need

Six celestite crystals, six tourmalines of various colours and a blue cloth. The crystals alternate around the body and all are placed point outwards. Celestite is put at the crown; one tourmaline either side of the head; at about shoulder level celestite is placed on either side; at mid arm, two tourmalines; close to the hands, two celestites and at calf level the remaining two tourmalines. The last celestite crystal is placed below and between the feet. All twelve crystals are evenly spaced around the body. You may use six different colours of tourmaline or some of one sort and some of another - the more colour, the more encompassing the experience.

What this net can be used for

Experiencing and exploring the qualities of blue light; increasing serenity and peacefulness; alignment to one's personal creative potential; ability to communicate and express; clearing the channels of personal expression and life-force; aligning oneself to finer levels of Higher Will; linking to the Master Energy of El Morya.

The energy of blue is to do with flow and communication on all levels from intergalactic to intracellular. Whenever and wherever there is a build-up of tension, frustration and blocking energies - there is the need for blue. Physically, blue light will quickly calm inflammation and other "hot" conditions like burns and arthritic aches. It is the antidote to an overconcentration of energy and as such is the polarity of red. The energy of blue works in the same way as water - it finds a common level for itself. Where there is imbalance, be it

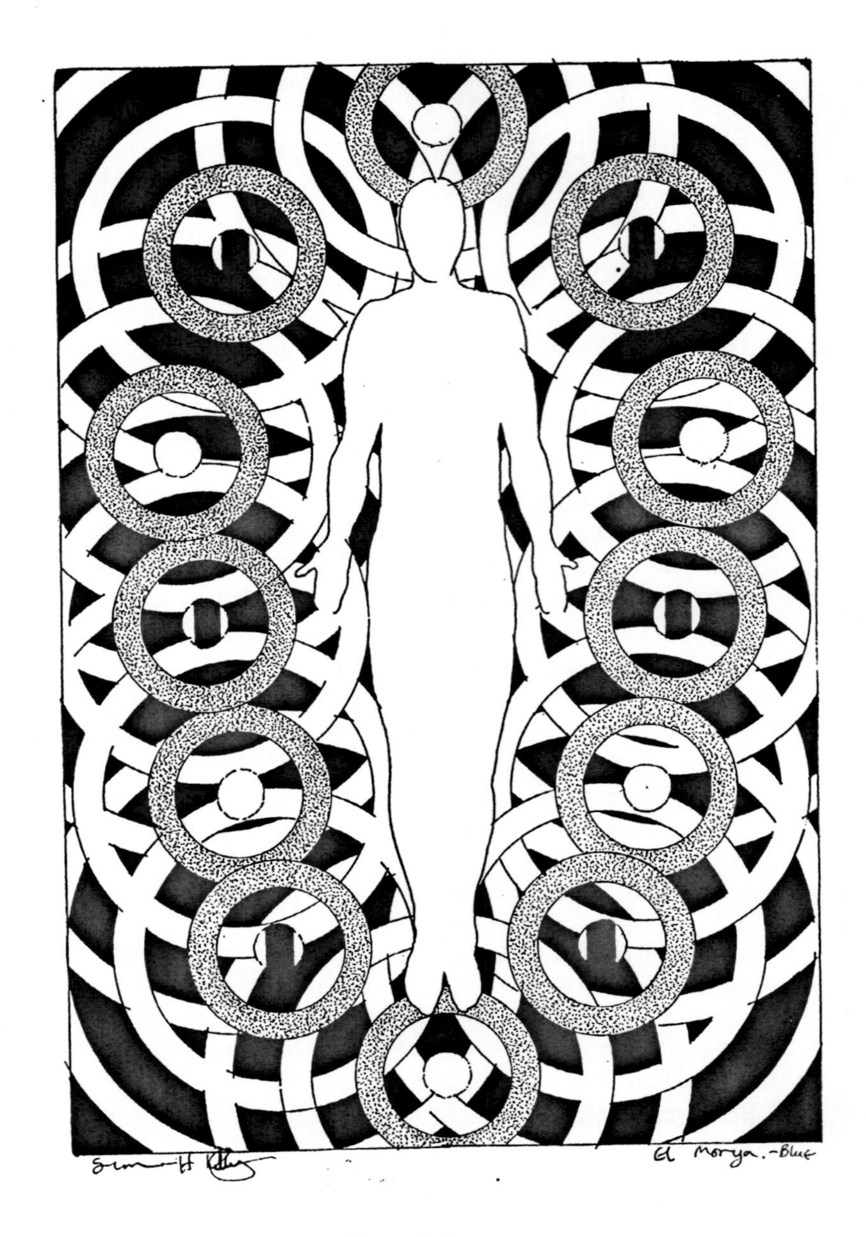

Blue - El Morya

overenthusiastic emotional responses or a head bursting with ideas and creativity, blue will help that pressure to release in a safe and constructive way.

Communication, of any sort, is a flow of information (or energy, or consciousness), from a place of high pressure to a place of lower pressure, from a place of greater knowledge to a place of lesser knowledge, be it on the spiritual level of master and disciple or on the level of gossip ("Have you heard about so and so?..").

Once the equalisation of energies has been accomplished there is peace. This is not the false peace of holding your breath and not daring to move in case of disturbing sleeping ogres, or acquiescing to another's wishes simply to avoid conflict. Peace is like a frictionless flow of energy-information between oneself and the universe, like the ever-moving currents within the ocean that can be felt but do not ripple the surface. Blue is vital for all intuitive processes, for the expression and elaboration of thoughts and for the communication of individuality and understanding.

The Master Key associated with blue is known as Morya or El Morya. He is said to be especially concerned with stimulating and energising "thought forms" (or ideas), of inspiring international ideals and far vision among statesmen and politicians. Morya manifests on the large scale as Will and Power positively working through state and government - that is, the expressive Will of a country and its people. Morya is historically associated with such figures as Akbar of India and Arthur of the Britons - those rulers who have attempted to integrate and strengthen their lands by cooperation rather than fear. In the individual, Morya represents the Higher Self that directs the desires and actions to achieve personal goals and fulfilment.

The ethereal light blue of celestite aptly encompasses the functions of this energy. It seems naturally to open one's awareness to fine levels of reality, whether that be a simple relaxation of tensions and worries or a visionary journey to angelic realms. In this net celestite is the communication channel to the universe whilst the tourmalines provide the anchors to integrate that information into the body for conscious understanding. The linear structure of the tourmaline also helps to focus celestite's "spacey" energy, and its electrical peculiarities make tourmaline a useful intermediary between the nervous system and the subtle levels of existence.

Violet - St. Germain

What you need

Eight amethyst crystals, if they have terminations, placed inwards: one above the head, one below the feet and the others spread evenly around the body. A yellow cloth.

What this net can be used for

Activating healing energy; freeing up personal potential; imagination and inspiration; integration of Spirit with Matter; understanding the relationship of cause and effect; attuning to the mechanics of ritual and ceremony; linking to the Master Energy of St. Germain.

The key to understanding violet energy is in the combination of its constituent colours, red and blue. Whereas purple is an equal admixture of those two colours, violet has proportionately more blue. There is little therapeutic difference between these two colours and these days the terms seem to be interchangeable. The important thing is that the colour, whatever it is called, is a union of heating, activating, dynamic manifesting red and cooling, sedating, pacifying, spiritualising blue. Thus violet is a spiritualisation of matter and an activation of spirit. It sums up the "*As above, so below...*" of Hermes Trimegistus and the image of the Ourobourus, the concept of microcosm reflecting macrocosm.

The healing action of violet/purple is in its balancing or completing of the spectrum. It is often thought of as the "spiritual" colour, usually by those who have an equal and opposite dislike for red - the dirty, worldly, sexy energy of matter! This simplistic duality, though rarely considered as

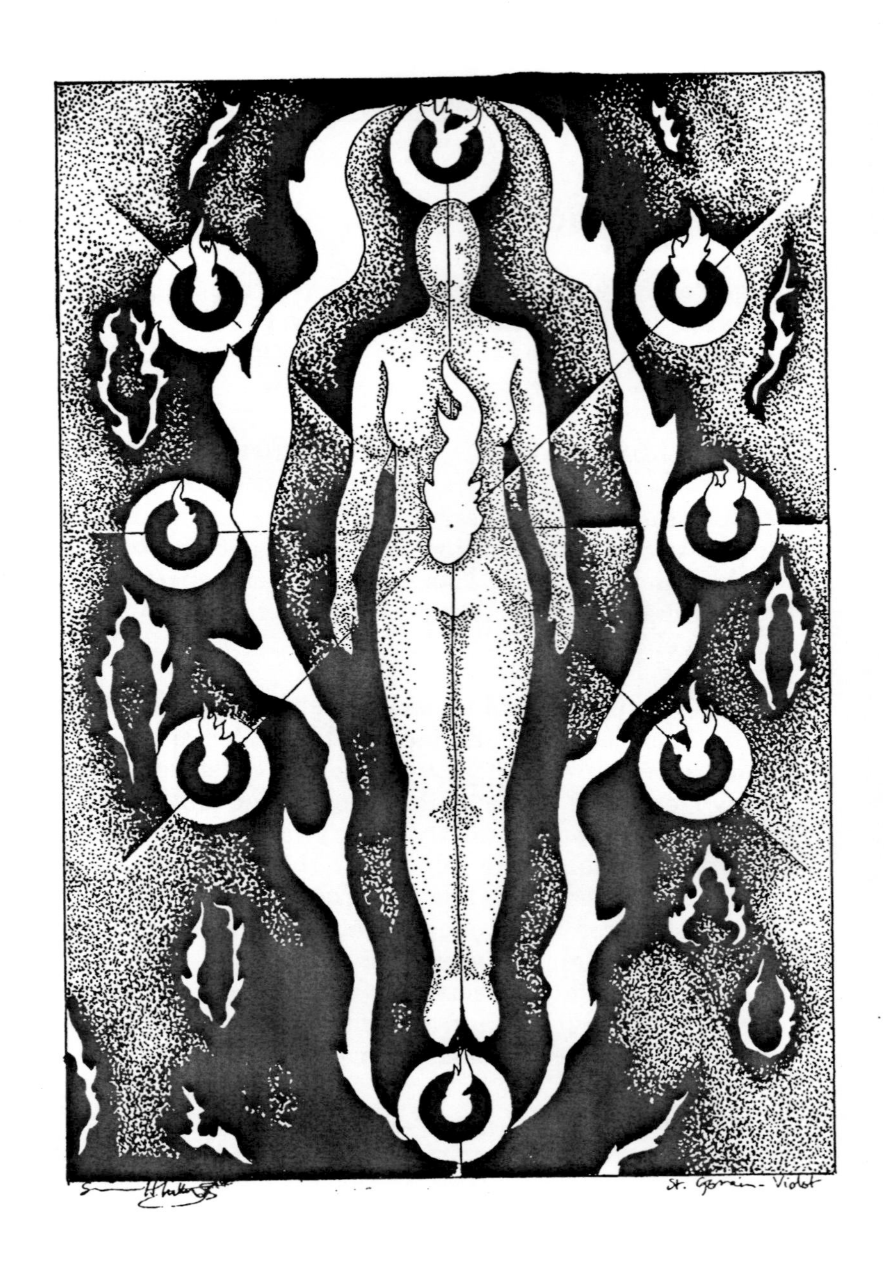

Violet - St Germain

such, is a thinly disguised Christian legacy where what is not godly is evil and what is not "spiritual" will lead straight to hell!

Violet is not superior or inferior to any other vibration, although people may have personal preferences to their experience of any given colour at the gut level (the body intelligence level). There is a historical, cultural superiority attached to purple as the production of dye from certain seashells was extremely costly and a well-guarded secret in the eastern Mediterranean city of Tyre. It was only able to be used ostentatiously by those with money, and in the Roman and Byzantine Empires strict rules were laid down as to how much purple could be worn indicating the social status of the individual and family. So wearing full purple assumed the political role of royalty - a role to which the colour in terms of its aspiration towards attainment of full potential and wholeness on every level, uniting heaven and earth, is, perhaps not coincidentally, completely apt.

Purple is associated with the workings of the imagination and the inspiration, and with symbolic form and ritual. The Master Key of this colour is known generally as St. Germain who is said to work on the 7th Ray of Ceremony and Magic. At first glance it looks peculiar and out of place to have a universal department dealing with this area of activity alone, but it is our own unusual cultural bias that makes it so.

Our society is almost entirely devoid of meaningful symbolic group activities and undervalues or misunderstands all symbolic activity be it art, play, dreaming or the reality of altered states of awareness. "It was only a dream", "It was only my imagination" has come to mean it was not real and therefore not valid.

In nearly every historical and every contemporary traditional society ceremony and magic are the lynch-pins of the community. They are not only the means to achieve social cohesion but they also uphold psychological and spiritual well-being. Ceremony and magic are the symbolic keys that explain to us the map of who we are and why we are here, and what needs to be done to maintain or improve our state. The centre of ceremony and magic is ritual, and the premise of ritual is that certain actions carried out in specific ways will bring about known, desired results that will benefit the individual or the society as a whole. It is now very difficult for us to see beyond the simplistic view of ritual as "sympathetic magic", working with the laws of cause and effect - a coercion of reality. Having been increasingly alienated from the world since we locked ourselves up behind city walls at the end of the neolithic period, we have lost the ability to see everything as a flow of interwoven energies.

Perhaps the closest we come today is in the symbolic energy known as money. The magicians juggling the patterns of interaction for the good of themselves or the communities they serve are economists and stockbrokers. Like former magicians and ritual priests they deal with intangibles - with things that "don't really exist" in the everyday world, but their actions have far-reaching and very tangible effects in almost all areas of life.

Ritual activity is the communication between different levels of energy or intelligence (blue), in order to bring about a manifestation of new physical states (red). It is the manipulation of matter (red) by means of the Will (blue), and by means of that careful handling what is desired comes about. That is, the red and the blue unite in a new form -purple.

Having looked at magic in this way we may understand a little better the activities of the Master of the Violet Ray, the mysterious St. Germain. In Alice Bailey he is the Master R., known as Rakoczi, Comte de St. Germain. In other books the spelling changes but the person remains the same - a mysterious diplomat, politician and aristocrat of Polish descent who moved through the courts of Europe during the turbulent latter half of the 18th century when Revolution was in the air. He apparently tried to curb some of the excesses of the ruling elite and gave warnings of the dire consequences should they fail to act in a more judicious way towards their citizens. His legendary status was ensured when he was seen in different places several years after he had supposedly been dead and buried. In fact, rumour had it that this same person had flitted through the centuries advising rulers and governments on their actions, disappearing and then reappearing again looking no older than when last seen decades before.

Whatever the reality, St. Germain represents those energies striving to evolve and unify on practical levels. Nowadays the concern is with economic growth and the political structure of society. The violet vibration works towards developing inner sensitivity and increasing the conscious awareness to understand greater levels of reality and also to see the Self as in equal partnership with all other aspects of creation. Its polarity vibration, golden yellow, under the patronage of Maat, is the basis of cosmic law and justice upon which the social ordering and structure of a fair, free society can be accomplished by the violet of St. Germain.

The energy of St. Germain is the imagination and the striving for fulfilled potential tempered by the balance of the Universal laws of nature, violation of which leads to fanatical megalomania and despotism. The amethyst layout for this net is identical to the Amethyst Healing Net except that the background vibration is yellow.

White - Serapis Bey

White - Serapis Bey

What you need

Six quartz crystals and six black tourmalines. A white or a black cloth. All crystal terminations should be turned out from the body, and all should be placed at least a handspan away from the body. One quartz is placed at the top of the head. Two more quartz are put either side of the throat and another two either side of the middle of the chest - about heart level. At the level of the navel on either side are two tourmalines and two more at the level of the mid-calf. The fifth tourmaline is put between and a little below the feet and the last tourmaline is in line with this but between one and two feet from the body. The sixth quartz crystal may either be positioned below these tourmalines or above the head, again between one or two feet from the top of the head. This variation will change the action of the net. When the quartz is placed above the crown the net focuses on a linking to the energies of white light at very subtle energy levels. When this stone is put below the feet there is much more of an emphasis on purification and cleansing energies.

What this net can be used for

Experiencing and understanding the qualities and properties of white light; links with Serapis Bey Master Energy; purification and cleansing; protection; renewal and rebirth.

White light symbolises the totality of existence before it becomes differentiated into the spectrum of colour. It thus represents wholeness and the source of light and life. White can both indicate a fullness or an emptiness - it possesses all colour within it yet has no colour visible. It can be all or nothing and as such it can be a disconcerting energy. Rather than explore the complexity and paradox inherent in white light the West has plumped for a straightforward " white is light is good and holy, black is darkness is bad and evil" polarisation. This over-simplification has stripped much symbolism of its power and has unleashed political correctness on the unsuspecting spectrum. It is not the only value judgement within the world of colour as there are other equally invidious distinctions made between "spiritual" and "base" colours. All however, should be studiously avoided if you wish to understand the essential power and energy of colour. Perhaps the surest way to come to your own conclusions about the qualities of black and white is to experience each within its own energy net.

White is energy experienced at its most actively complete, and is associated with the solar light in many of its associative forms: creative, life-giving, clarifying, dispelling the unknown, revealing, enlightening and so on. The Key Master energy expressing the essence of white reflects these qualities and is known to us as Serapis Bey. The name sounds a bit like an Ottoman Egyptian potentate where "bey" is a title of esteem like "sir" or "lord". Serapis, however, has a long and mysterious history deriving from the Dynastic Egyptian Mysteries.

One of the most sacred places in ancient Egypt was the Serapeum - the temple of Serapis and the dwelling place of the sacred Apis bulls. Serapis was a composite god, blending the creative aspects of Ptah with the generative aspects of Asar (Osiris). He appeared as the great figure of a goat-headed or bull-headed man. On the physical level Asar-Apis manifested in the Apis bulls. These bulls were identified by a series of very specific markings on their bodies. Once recognised they lived in the temple itself and were worshipped as an incarnation of Ptah, and a representation of the creative powers of the sun's fire brought to earth. If the bulls lived beyond a certain age they were ritually killed, mummified and buried in giant pink granite sarcophagi. Once dead, the Apis bull carried the sun's energy to Osiris, god of death and rebirth, where the power could be assimilated into the land itself and renew its fertility and strength. The Serapeum was the spiritual battery of Egypt. It was where the continuity of regeneration, purification and rebirth were maintained. The Apis bulls represented life at its most powerful and virile, their presence, both alive and dead, fertilised the soul of Egypt.

Alice Bailey has little to say about Serapis Bey, or "The Egyptian", except that his work is related to the evolution of art and music and that he was primarily concerned with the evolution of higher beings who would, in turn, influence artistic activity. Even here then, we see a link to creativity within the white vibration. It is the expression of the energy of potential, and manifestation of potential upon every level of creation.

If your creative source, your soul, is blocked in any way, or the well that feeds the richness of your life appears to be dry, this net will help to put you in touch again with your potential. Be advised however, that white is not a timid energy and the block removal and purification may be a little more forceful than you would have expected!

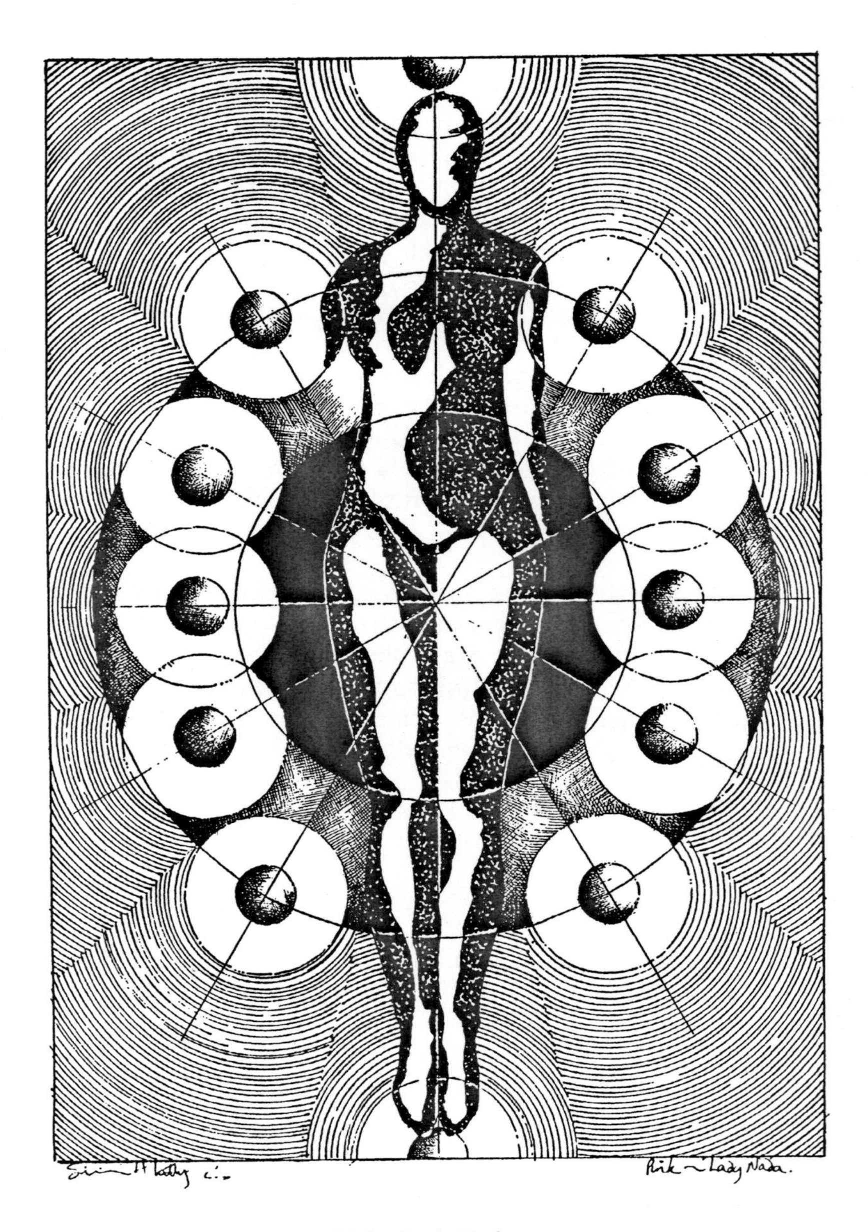

Pink - Lady Nada

Pink - Lady Nada

What you need

Twelve rose quartz, tumbled or natural stones, placed evenly spaced around the body. A mid-pink or dark-pink cloth.

What this net can be used for

All issues to do with self-worth, self-confidence, self-acceptance and so on; connecting with universal levels of love and compassion; understanding of unity in diversity, and so therefore tolerance, forgiveness and clarity of being; all aspects of nurturing and creativity; fine and finest levels of consciousness and the connectedness of consciousness throughout the universe; subtle aspects of sound and vibration.

There are three nets and three Master energies that vibrate to different aspects of the colour pink. The Nada energy can be seen as the most fundamental and all-pervading, whilst the other two energies focus various protective and creative aspects of the colour.

Pink is the combination of white and red and so can be nothing if not dynamic. However, as white is the totality of expression within the spectrum, so the dynamism of pink will be equally spread throughout all of creation. That is, pink is not necessarily a very obvious vibration - one has to look beneath the apparent surface to see it. At its most fundamental level Nada IS vibration, it is matter and is consciousness. In Sanskrit "nada" means sound, and sound is held to be the initiating principle in creation. It is the movement on the face of the waters that begins the process of recognition of Self and not-Self, and of the vast interplay of this exploration of existence - the Universe both manifest and subtle. Nada is what holds everything together - it is the glue of the universe, the unifying principle that, when everything else has been divided down to the basic building blocks of matter, there is nothing but the vibration of energy and the interplay of the waves that energy creates within itself.

Pink is unconditional energy. Because it is the reality behind the mask of creation, everything is understood in terms of its real nature, which is unified: one ocean with billions of individual waves. Once this is understood all divisions, jealousies, aggressive acts, misunderstandings fade away. Pink isn't a lovey-dovey soft energy, it is an uncompromising knowledge of reality. As such it is the best colour to use where any aggression or negative influences are present. Short exposure to deep pink light has been used to great effect in prisons when riots threaten to erupt and also in police cells to calm violent drunks. Visualising pink light from one's own heart outwards dispels negativity, and projecting pink around or at someone who is either aggressive towards you or who you cannot get on with calms any situation down before it gets out of hand.

Unconditional love, the nature of pink, is not an emotion, a mood or a wishful thought. It is what we call that state of complete union with Reality As It Is. It is not something that can be explained, understood or experienced in terms of relative existence. Only when the individual has formed an unbreakable bond with the underlying experience of consciousness and sees no duality ie. a being who has become enlightened, can this state be said to be known and lived. Everything else is moodmaking and ego deceit.

In this state of unconditional love there is true compassion, an understanding of the whole picture of the universe and the ability to act for the good of all. This state doesn't stem from an intellectual knowledge of infinite facts but it is because the individual in this state is no longer an individual at all. The wave has become the ocean, though still existing in form as the wave.

More than wishing is needed to understand the reality of Unconditional Being, but the Nada net may help us to tune in (literally), to the all-pervading vibration of creation.

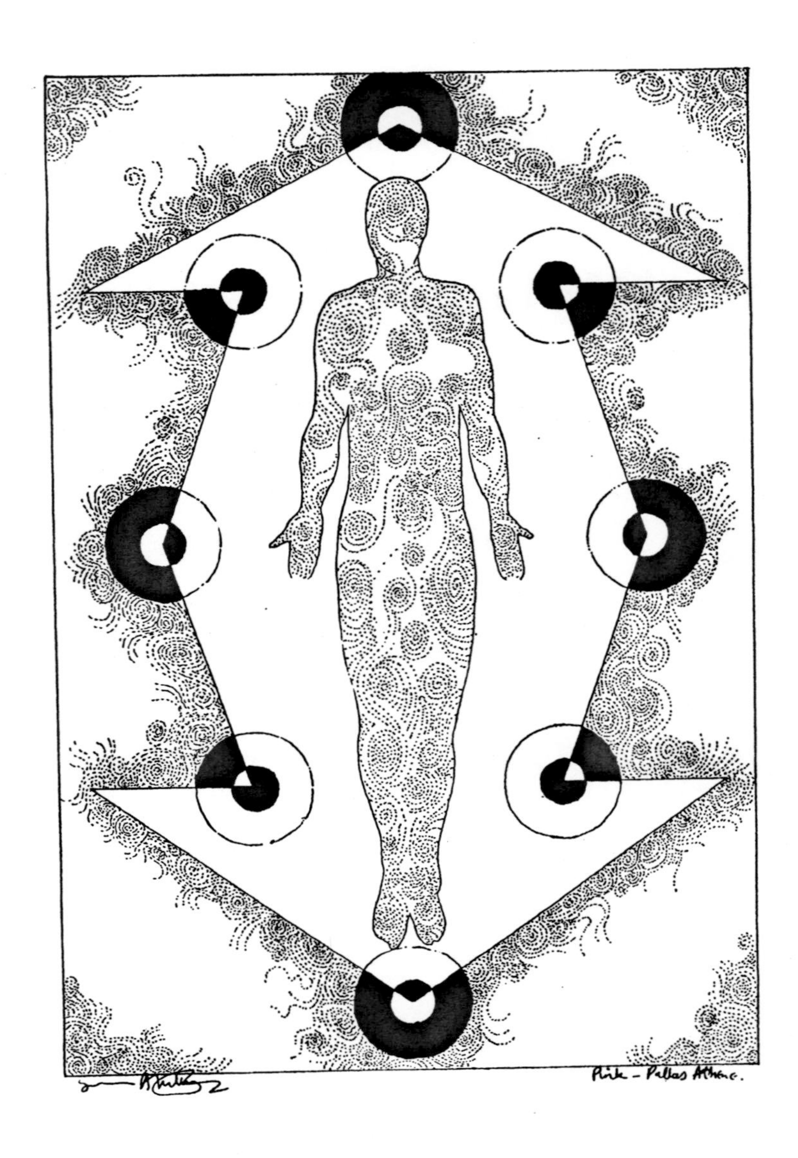

Magenta-pink - Pallas Athene

Magenta-pink - Pallas Athene

What you need

Eight clear quartz crystals, points outwards, evenly spaced around the body. A deep pink cloth.

What this net can be used for

Creating protected space; equilibrium; calming fears and anxieties; creative assertiveness; understanding the natural laws of manifestation; balancing polarities, male and female.

The shade of pink this net addresses and the Master Energy it activates is a rich colour akin to magenta. It is a pink with more of the active red energy about it and so is a more dynamic vibration. The archetypal role is the protectress, the guardian mother, the nurturer of her offspring. This aspect of the Goddess can be found in various guises around the world. Pallas Athene is the name we know this energy by, and her story indicates quite clearly the characteristics of the vibration.

Athene has been traced back by way of Minoan Crete to Libya where a triple snake goddess Neith, (also known to the Egyptians) held powerful sway. Many of Pallas Athene's attributes - guardian snake, Medusa mask, goatskin and snake breastplate - hark back directly to the worship of the Goddess as Neith. The olive tree, Athene's gift to the city of Athens, was originally imported from the lands of Libya. Her Classical image, known to us from the works of later sculptors, shows Athene as a majestic woman wrapped in tight draperies and clad in armour. She holds a spear and shield, has a crested helmet on her head and wears the "aegis", a breastplate of goatskin edged by snakes with the Gorgon's head in the centre. She is accompanied by a large serpent and an owl, signifying prophecy and wisdom.

Pallas Athene is actually two goddesses conjoined. There are several Classical stories that give different explanations of the name, and various authorities have suggested their own ideas. Essentially "Pallas" translates as either "maiden warrior" or "young male warrior" depending on how the word is pronounced. The gist of the tales suggest Pallas was a warrior goddess introduced with the patrilinear Greek peoples as they moved west into what is now Greece. She became integrated with the matrifocal goddess Athena, a household goddess whose name is so old it is impossible to translate.

So the goddess assumes the role of another on her way to becoming the primary goddess of the Greek culture - a culture which preferred to suppress the goddess religions in hopes of patrilinear control. Thus the attributes that survive (up-front at least, as it were), are those acceptable to the new regime. The legend of Athene springing fully armed from Zeus's forehead, (her mother having been swallowed, or culturally absorbed, by the Father god), avoids her having to be born by a mother, thus neatly ending the primacy of the Goddess lineage in favour of the gods. As she is also fiercely chaste and a formidable warrior she can be worshipped as a female man.

Pallas Athene has also been seen as an amalgamation of the ancient Libyan triple goddess, where Pallas is the maiden, Athene the nurturing mother and Medusa the wise old woman. Then in the Greek "hostile takeover" there is the inevitable "rationalisation" where those aspects not required by the patriarchal system are dumped or disguised. Hence the powerful, seductive aspect of the Medusa - the snake/ wisdom/ sex aspect - is slain by the brave Perseus with Athene's own help, and the Gorgon's powers are thenceforth controlled by Athene, placed on her breastplate to turn her own and her people's enemies to stone.

A further footnote to this transformation and assimilation process is that the "Palladium", the sacred focus for the city of Athens, associated with Pallas, is either thought to have been a likeness of the warrior maiden of that name accidentally killed by the goddess or a phallic image of the warrior/fertility god!

Whatever the historical and cultural tides going on here, in terms of energy what we see is an assimilation of conflicting cultural models and belief systems into one all-powerful goddess fiercely protective of her city and its people. Pallas Athene becomes the bestower of the civilising influences of culture, the acceptable goddess/female/woman's work skills protected by the heroic/male/warrior all rolled into one deity. Pallas Athene was said to have invented the flute, the trumpet, the potter's wheel, earthenware vases, the plough, the rake and the ox-yoke. She is patroness of artists, crafts-people, architects, smiths and metalworkers and at the same time keeps an eye on all cooks, embroiderers, woodworkers and weavers. This list of patronage, to which can be added health and healing, is a clear demonstration of what creativity can be revealed when male-female, analytical-intuitive, active-passive roles of polarity are integrated and harmonised in one being. Putting aside the evolution and manipulation of the imagery, at its fundamental level, the energy of Pallas Athene transcends all superficial gender issues and expresses the self-assured, creative, protective wholeness of the universe.

Consider using this net when you appear to be pulled in several directions at once or when your sense of personal space and creativity is being blocked by other's wishes. Where there are problems with family history, abuse, misunderstanding, insecurity, this net will help to remove the stress whilst encouraging a supporting understanding of all sides.

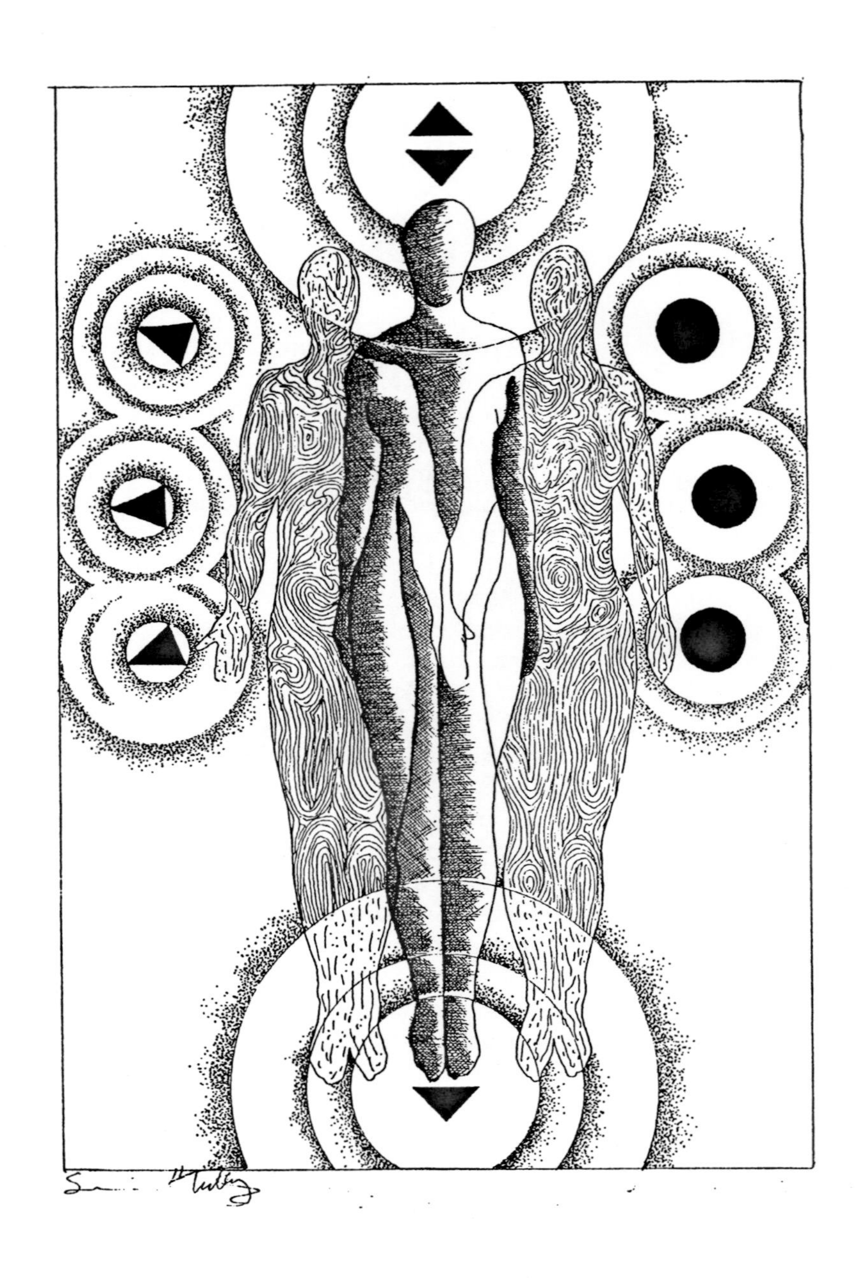

Pale blue - pale pink - Orion and Angelica

Pale blue - pale pink: Orion and Angelica

What you need

Three rose quartz, three celestite crystals, three smoky quartz and a pale pink cloth. The smoky quartz is placed on the central axis of the body - one at the crown is placed point down; a second is placed above this with point upwards (ie. away from the body); the third quartz is placed below the feet point away from the body. The three rose quartz crystals are all placed on the left side of the body at neck/shoulder level, solar plexus level and hip level. Opposite these stones on the right side of the body, put the celestite crystals, point outwards if they have terminations.

What this net can be used for

To connect with the Earth as a planetary being; overview of time-cycles; balancing of polarities; understanding creation - destruction, loss and rebirth; helpful where there are endings and beginnings, whether positive or difficult; protective and supporting; links to awareness beyond the solar system.

This energy vibration has no clear correlation in either colour or Master Energy hierarchies. As far as we are aware the names were attributed to a particular protecting energy entering the Earth's sphere from elsewhere in the cosmos - and as such Orion and Angelica is an extra-terrestrial vibration. However, remembering that all types of energy vibration are equally accessible wherever they may be perceived in time and space, there is nothing "alien" about this energy.

Orion and Angelica can be seen as being like dawn and sunset or like the morning and evening stars. This brings to mind the Twin Gods of the morning and evening stars worshipped in the Middle East before the rise of Hebraic monotheism.

Star gods were very important to a great many ancient civilisations, and especially relevant here is the belief of the Egyptians. With our current worldview we tend to see Dynastic Egypt as a rather quirky one-off, yet immensely fascinating, period of history whilst forgetting that it was THE formative culture for the development of European cultures. Its existence was so stable and productive that it is perhaps more accurate to see Egypt as our cultural and philosophical home, rather than the much later Classical Greece and Rome who were taught nearly all they knew by Egyptian priest-philosophers. In Egypt the primary stellar deities, apart from the Sun, were the constellation we know as Orion and the star that follows it across the sky, Sirius.

The appearance of these stars over the horizon marked the beginning of the yearly inundation of the Nile and with it the farming year. Orion was seen as the god Asar (Osiris), and Sirius, his sister-wife Asat (Isis). Asar and Asat are viewed as a very human sort of deity - as mother and father gods. The world over which they ruled was one of harmony and abundance. They were credited with teaching the skills of agriculture and husbandry to mankind. Asar (Osiris) was eventually slain by his jealous brother Set and one of the most poignant of all Egyptian myths is of Asat (Isis), travelling in mourning throughout the world to find the hiding places of the dismembered parts of her husband. Asat magically restores Asar to life and Horus, the Hawk, their avenging son is conceived before Asar returns to the land of the dead as its king and guardian.

Osiris and Isis are always portrayed in fully human form, fairly unusual for Egyptian deities, and Osiris-Asar has green skin. On one level he is the original Green Man, the spirit of vegetation that dies and is reborn each year by the power of the inundation of the Nile, presaged by the appearance of the star Sirius - the visible form of Asat-Isis, Queen of Heaven, who is ever following her love Asar-Osiris-Orion across the night skies.

As cultural patrons, Asar and Asat are fitting prototypes for the creative, protective, guardian energies represented by Orion and Angelica.

The combination and placement of stones in this net are unusual and interesting. The axis of smoky quartz works like a central focus and grounding. They allow a protected space that links both to the Earth and the cosmos and helps to reveal or manifest the hidden aspects of creation, which the Asar-Osiris energy represents. The remaining rose quartz and celestite stones create a gentle polarity of warm-cool, active-passive, male-female, as Asar and Asat, too, embody those fundamental halves within our own selves.

Astrological nets

The most individual and personal of energy nets are those derived from the natal astrological chart. The position of the planets at birth is an important blueprint for each life time. It shows the relationship of the universal energies to the individual. The natal chart can be seen as a toolkit for that life. It shows skills, timings, gifts and contradictions that, to develop full potential, the individual needs to explore and master.

Each zodiac sign symbolises an aspect of universal energy influencing life, creating a background or energy backdrop. Where there is a planet or sensitive point located in a sign on a birth chart, the planet or point acts as a sort of lens that focuses and concentrates the background influences in a specific way. The planet or sensitive point represents an archetypal drive within an individual, the sign that is the backdrop shows how the drive will tend to be used. (Put sunlight through a red filter and it will look red - it is still sunlight, but focussed on a small part of the spectrum. Shine the stellar influence of Pisces, for example, through the lens of the Moon onto the Earth, and the qualities of Moon will be flavoured by Pisces).

These drives shown by the natal chart interlink with one another to create particular traits or habits. Sometimes these influences are easier to cope with than others, but it is important to remember that none are "better" or "worse" than others. A "difficult" combination can be a thorn in the side or a goad to get up out of the briar bush - depending on your attitude. Conversely, so-called "easy" combinations create such an easy flow of energy, it can prove difficult to focus that flow in a conscious way.

To set up such a personal astrological net and use it on a regular basis would reaffirm the personal signature of energies capable of being drawn on at any one time, as well as strengthening personal identity.

Once you have access to natal chart data, either choose, dowse or muscle-test for crystals to match the signs, planets and houses, appropriate for the individual chart. (See Appendices 2 and 4).

Then, place the stones, where appropriate,(matching the placement on the natal chart) in a circle or ellipse around the body.

Although we have found "head to north" seems appropriate in most cases, it is worth experiencing the net with the "head to south" orientation.

If there are particularly difficult areas within the chart, emphasis can be placed on these, both to experience and to understand the conflicting energies - and to modify and harmonise the tensions.

Most astrological stresses have a release point that an astrologer will be able to recognise. Once this point is known, suitable stones and net can be used to activate the release.

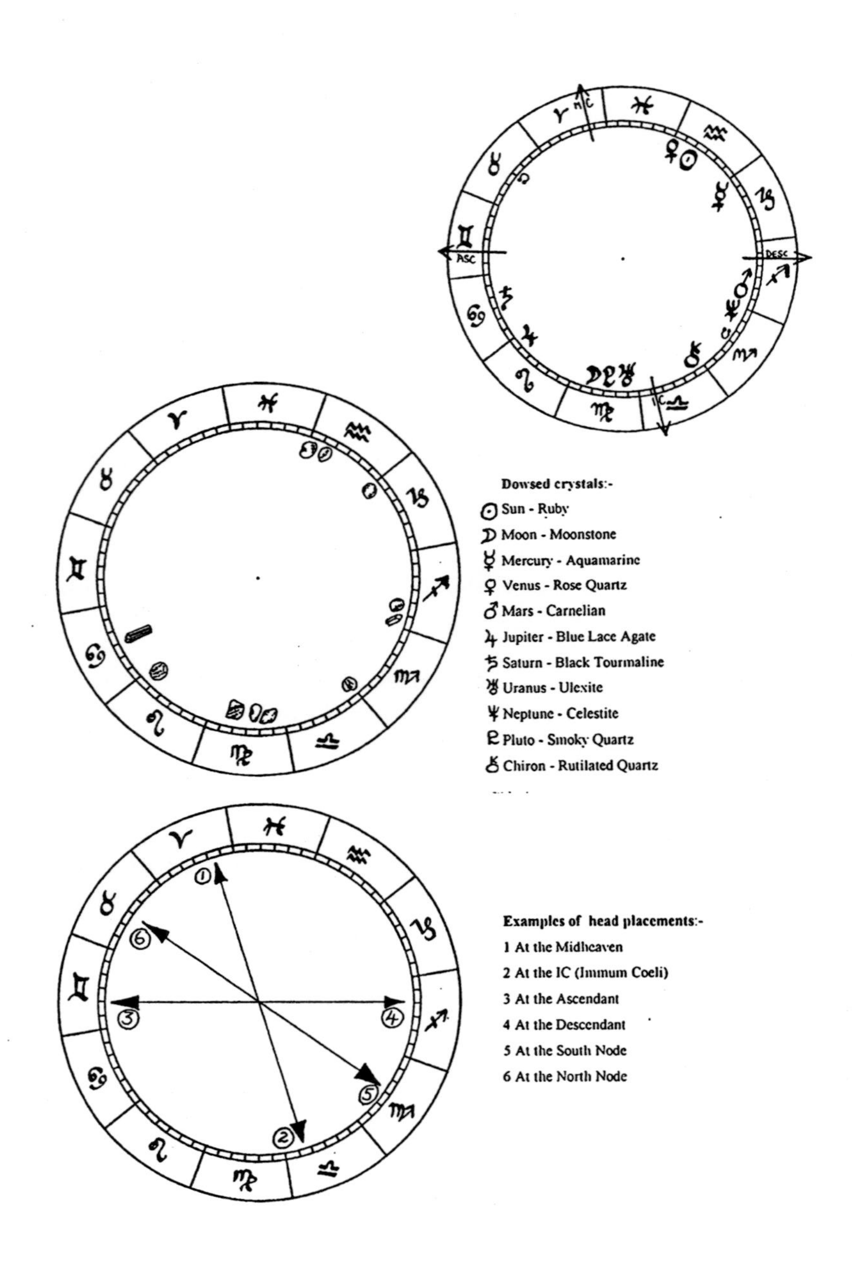

Example of a natal chart

Working with nets for astrological transits

The natal chart is a representation of energy patterns present at birth.

However, the universal energies represented by the signs, planets and so on, are continually changing relationships with each other, and at certain times the new patterns will impinge on the natal blueprint.

Such triggering occurs, for example, when a planet (in real time),passes over, or transits, the angle or position of the same or another planet in the natal blueprint.

Many transits go almost unnoticed, but a few can reflect major upheavals in lifestyle, attitude and experience. Foreknowledge of these can, using energy nets, be worked on and experienced before it happens in "real time". This allows the energy systems of the body to acclimatise to new conditions and new stresses, ultimately enabling the energies to be used more creatively.

During the period of a transit, nets can help to encourage the acceptance of new circumstances in a positive and helpful way. Nets can help to create a window of time, allowing the individual to integrate the new energies. Sometimes transits can be very intense and it is useful to have a period of respite, when the net can produce a sort of "Faraday Cage", to create a detached space to encourage contemplation and self-reflection.

Absent healing with nets

Whilst it is always better to work with the person present, sometimes it isn't possible. Working with energy nets absently, provides an excellent tool for healing and for the development of personal potential.

Absent work tends to require slightly longer exposure than if a person is present in the net. It is essential that the person being worked on is aware of the exact time that the net is set up and is prepared. It might be thought of as unethical to work on people without their permission.

What is required is a "witness" - something that links the net to the individual. Typical witnesses are a small sample of hair, saliva or blood, but it is equally effective to use a sample of handwriting (particularly a signature) or just the name written out. A body outline drawn on a sheet of paper around which stones can be placed is a useful addition. You can use as a background a cloth of an appropriate colour (silk or felt squares are excellent), a plain mirror-glass surface or crystal slab.

A natal astrological chart can be used for absent work. An A4 copy of a chart is probably the best workable size. You would not necessarily need a witness if you have an accurate chart, as this is a witness by itself. Crystals can be placed around the chart where appropriate. You can choose what and where to place certain stones, or you can dowse or muscle-test. Visual contemplation of nets set out in this way can be a useful personal exercise, particularly when used with the astrological and personal energy nets. The presence of the layout will act as a reinforcing message while the visual contact allows colour and gemstone energies direct access, via the eyes, to the hypothalamus and other controlling organs within the brain.

It is best to remember that when working absently you need to ensure that you are grounded and focussed. (See Appendix 5)

If you are leaving the absent work in place for a period of time, it would need to be in a place where it is not disturbed and where it doesn't disrupt the use of any living space.

Templates for healing - chakra templates

The chakra system has become one of the better known models for working with human subtle anatomies, both in healing and spiritual development. The system first became known to the West through 19th and 20th century translations of Indian treatises, especially from the Tantric schools of Northern India. These texts described seven main wheels of energy (chakra= wheel) aligned along the spine and appearing as various coloured spinning vortices of energy. Each chakra was related to specific colours, sounds, deities, qualities of experience, behaviour patterns and overall states of health. In these original sources we do not find the simple, single colour rainbow sequence from red to violet which is prevalent in the descriptions today. Despite this, the latter correlation of chakra with colour is an effective addition to the scheme, making it easier to remember the functions of colour vibration and chakra energy.

There is not the space here to delve deeply into chakra theory but there are some important points to bear in mind before examining each chakra and template in more detail.

Firstly, a vortex is formed when two or more streams of energy meet together. Each chakra is therefore the site where many different energy flows interact within the human being. Although most diagrams show chakras on the line of the spinal column from base to crown, there is a complex interaction between each centre.

Chakras could equally be viewed in terms of a solar system, or as electrons around an atom or as interpenetrating spheres of energy where every change effects and augments the function of every other sphere. There are numerous other chakras apart from these major seven: below the body, above the head, within the physical body, within the aura, all of which have specific functions and characteristics.

Certainly each chakra is multidimensional, not limited to traditional views and senses attributed to it, and each can be viewed as a world in its own right - a living being on another scale. As such it can be imprudent to wish to change the state of any chakra to one that an individual may perceive as being more "evolved".

As we cannot ever be consciously aware of what is going on at every level of each chakra's functioning it is important when working with these energies to set the parameters for our goals in terms of the overall balance and stability of the system as a whole. Otherwise we may find we have an enlightened head in a completely blown out and fused body.

The chakras transmit the life-force into the body, not only from our immediate environment but also from the soul, the complete spiritual essence of who we are, and from every other energy source in the universe (the "all pervasive sources"). Through these dynamic centres energy is distributed into the rest of the energy system via the subtle channels or nerves known as "nadis".

The seven main chakras are related physically to major endocrine glands and ganglia of nerve and lymphatic tissue that in some way echo the state of the chakra's energy. Malfunction or disease in a particular part of the body can be related back to the nearest chakras but it is important to remember that the chakra system is completely integrated and finely balanced and if there is imbalance in one area there is going to be a corresponding imbalance in other areas as well.

There is a very common and dubious belief that the "lower" chakras (i.e. those below the heart) are somewhat dirty and smutty, dealing with things like the gross physical world, sex, and all those difficult desires for unspiritual things. Correspondingly, those chakras above the heart are only to do with spirit, evolution, enlightenment and all the worthy human attributes and wish-fulfilments. This view is a persistent anachronism from neurotic, guilt-ridden 19th century Christian Western Europe. Happiness and enlightenment cannot be gained by ignoring the physical reality of here and now. If we weren't to work with the dust and dirt we wouldn't need to be here on this world at all. If we fail to address the transformation and growth of ALL aspects of our reality then we will not get anywhere, except in a self-deluded mess.

There is also the common misconception of "opening" and "closing" chakras. Firstly if a chakra is closed completely you will find yourself without a body to live in (!) and if you open wide a chakra you may well blow more fuses that you can fix, or attract some energy-hungry being (physical or otherwise) who will play havoc with your life and enjoy every moment of your discomfort. The term "shutting down" a chakra is usually meant to signify: returning to normal parameters of function, or sometimes, protecting the energy field from unwanted attention. The development of sequential opening or cleansing of chakras happens naturally as a result of personal growth, it is not itself the means of achieving any permanent change in awareness.

Within the boundaries of normal functioning some chakras will be more active than others and when working with crystal energies, meditation and ritual it is advisable to consciously WILL the chakras to return to everyday balance before resuming normal activities. This prevents the spiritual equivalent of walking into a crowded street with your flies undone to cries of "We know what you've been doing!".

The chakra templates described here naturally augment the functioning of each chakra and supply a boost of appropriate energy which may allow blocks of energy to be more easily removed and so to encourage healing. Alternatively working with a template may temporarily focus your consciousness in a way harmonious to that energy field and by this means you might find yourself in a "lift" between different levels of awareness, exploring the structures of worlds within.

Because chakras are so vital to the energy integrity of our bodies we recommend you use dowsing or muscle-testing techniques to determine the most appropriate template to use at any one time. These templates are not designed to be used all at once - becoming a mosaic floor will not further your life purpose. It may be appropriate to use two or three templates simultaneously in some circumstances, though we have found it more likely that there will be a sequence of templates to be done in a specific order each for a definite number of minutes. Guidelines for using chakra templates are the same as for energy nets, please remember to follow them.

Base chakra template

Base chakra template

What you need

Four clear quartz crystals placed diagonally in a square, with points outwards. Between these crystals forming another square (this time along vertical and horizontal axes of the body), four dark tourmalines with terminations outwards. A red, brown or black stone placed in the centre of these two squares (dowse or muscle-test for the most appropriate kind).

What this template is used for

Balancing and augmenting the base chakra functions; survival, for centreing and grounding; increased energy; motivation; increased circulation; focus on practicality; counters disorientation;relaxation of physical body; stress; problems with legs, feet, large intestine, arthritis, physical existence.

The Base Chakra is located at the base of the spine. In Sanskrit it is known as "Muladhara", which means "root" or "support". The template can be arranged anywhere between the pubic bone, groin and the upper knees depending on the size of the crystals and the shape of your body. Some stones can be off the physical body, some on the body or a combination of these. You might find you will need some micropore tape to secure the stones in place.

The Base Chakra is vital to the functioning of the individual on every level. It is the foundation upon which all the other energy centres rely for stability and is the major source of useable energy. If the Base Chakra is not functioning well there will be a feeling of unreality, not belonging, not being able to cope, not being able to do anything and though other chakras might function they will not be able to manifest their reality into the physical world, that is they will be completely useless. The energy expressed by the Muladhara is solidity, the concretion of form, the experience of existence, the reality of matter and how to use it, the principle of survival. The equivalent colour vibration is red.

Sacral chakra template

What you need

Placed between the navel and the pubic bone; three clear crystals of the same type in a downward pointing triangle, points outwards. Suitable crystals would be three of either clear quartz, rutilated quartz, diamond or herkimer diamond. (Dowse for best). Below this is an arc of three stones all the same sort, with the lowest point nearest the pubis, of either of the following: moonstone,rose quartz,lapis lazuli, aquamarine, sugilite, amethyst, charoite, blue quartz.

What this template can be used for

Balancing and augmenting the Sacral Chakra; easing sexual tension and problems; bladder or kidney troubles; low back pain; impotence and frigidity; stabilising emotions; clarifying sense of self in relation to others; sensuality; detoxification; arthritic conditions;skeletal problems; anger; frustration; aggression; anxiety about self-image; creativity; pleasure.

The Second Chakra, known as the Sacral or Sexual Chakra is called "Svadhisthana" in Sanskrit, meaning "sweetness". It is located in the lower abdomen between the navel and the pubic bone, though in celibates its functions divert to the area of the spleen.

Whereas the Base Chakra is related to earth and the stillness of solidity, the Sacral Chakra is linked to the movement and flow of energy. It is the desire for the Other (the not-Self) which makes the Self reach out and move towards what it desires. This movement is the essential characteristic of all energy and interaction, and the cause of it is desire for pleasure. Pleasure is not something which is only grabbed

Sacral chakra template

whilst nobody is looking - it is the reason for existence in the first place. An experience of pleasure means that the body is in a relaxed and balanced state, free of fear and stress. Pleasure will remain until there is a change of state and then we must move on to find a new state of harmony, a new feeling of pleasure.

Many years ago a Sunday paper ran a series of articles on research just then completed examining the function of pathways in the developing brain. One of the conclusions found that the baby, child, adult would always seek those experiences that would stimulate the pleasure areas of the brain - the limbic system. The whole tone of the report suggested that it was all rather shocking and perhaps even demeaning that humans were "only" interested in enjoying themselves. Surely we are in a sorry state if we feel nervous about this revelation. And the fact that we had to pay scientists to discover what we should have been aware of all along is a revealing indictment of what a mess urban 20th century western civilisation has become and how far we have suppressed the natural energies of the Sacral Chakra.

Once desire and motivation is restricted/suppressed, consciousness has nowhere to flow, creativity dries up, boredom stagnates us and we begin to fear change, the one thing that will stimulate us to a sweeter life. Tension and fear begins to alienate us from ourselves and our environment and energy gets blocked where it doesn't belong, causing illness and disease. Any physical, emotional, mental or spiritual stiffness or constipation suggests you might benefit from work on your Sacral Chakra, whose equivalent colour is orange.

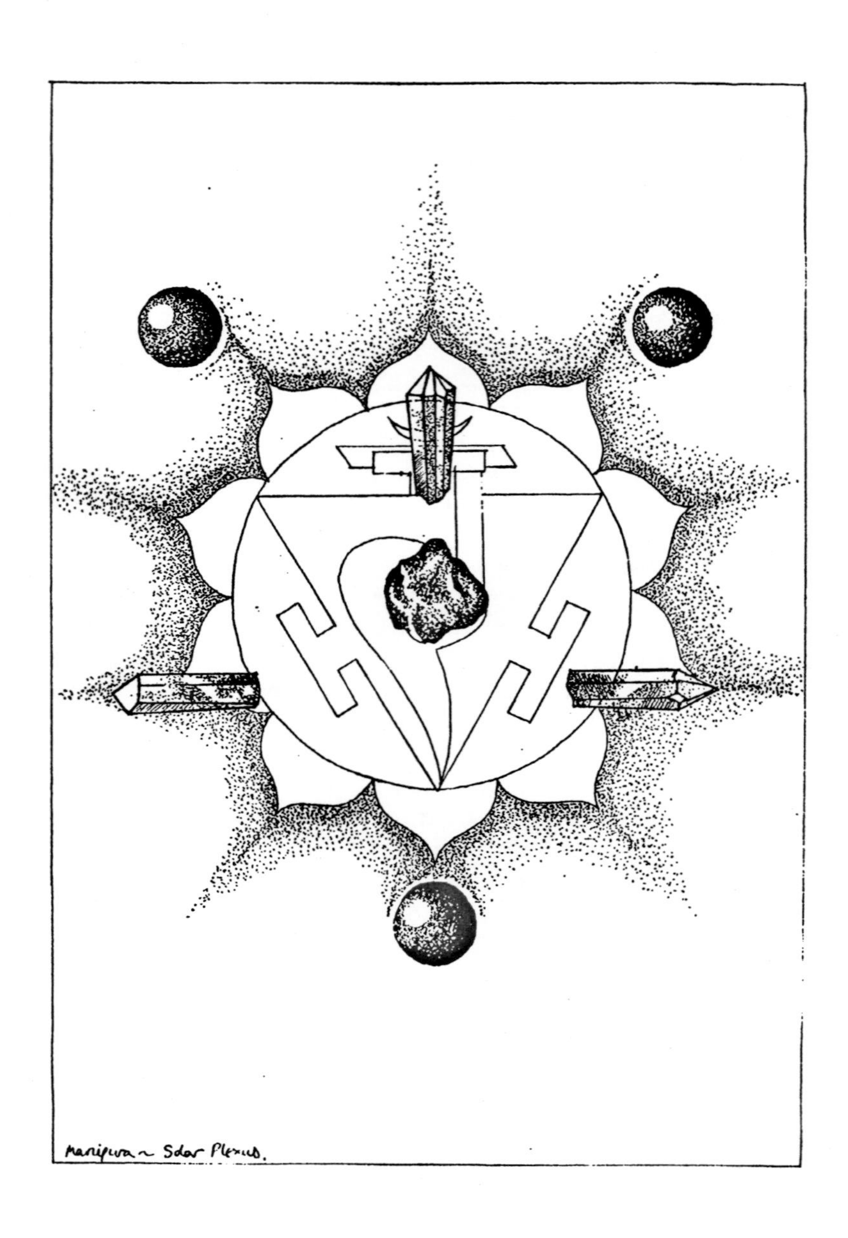

Solar plexus chakra template

Solar plexus chakra template

What you need

Between the lower edge of the ribcage, near the diaphragm, and the navel: an upward-pointing triangle of citrine quartz (with points outwards). In the centre of this triangle, one stone of either tiger's eye, ruby, garnet, jasper or pyrites. Three garnets making an outer downward-pointing triangle surrounding the other stones.

What this template can be used for

Balancing and augmenting solar plexus chakra functions; sense of personal power and ability; joy, laughter, spontaneity; self-confidence; digestion of nutrients; helps fight chronic infections and digestive disorders; strengthens immune system; fear of weakness; inability to release stress; balances nervous system.

This chakra is called "Manipura" - "lustrous gem". It relates to the element of fire and is concerned with the use of energy and the ability to transform energy into a new level of dynamism within the individual's system. It gives the power to organise and create new states both internally and in the world. As such it is related to Power and Will. This centre has so much to do with our relationship to the "outside" world that it can become quite easily exhausted. The Solar Plexus deals on many levels with the ability to recognise and identify the uses of energy from sources other than "us". When it functions well we can easily transform "not self" into "self" to feed our Being.

When the Manipura chakra becomes unbalanced we quickly lose sense of direction, lose our ability to deal with life in a spontaneous, creative way. Stress and inhibitions accumulate forcing us either to inaction and apathy or into overcompensation by driving ourselves to a workaholic, perfectionist, stomach-melting frenzy. Within the Solar Plexus region is the diaphragm, controlling depth of breathing. If you have lot of stress in this area you may find that this template will make you take deep, full breaths, sighs or yawns as the knots of tensions begin to release. The small intestine, stomach and liver all work to transform external matter; identifying what is of use to the body and absorbing it as nutrients. In the same area the spleen plays an important role in the body's immunity - another system that relies on the ability to recognise what is useful and what is harmful to the organism.

This chakra also plays an important role in other "self - not-self" barriers, like the skin and nervous system. As a major fuse-box in the body's energy systems it is usually fairly apparent when something blows: immune system compromise, over-acidity, ulcers, digestive problems, malabsorption of nutrients, anxiety and stress, constant colds, insecurity, lack of confidence, hypertension, "burn-out". In fact a great majority of 20th century malaise can be traced to imbalance in the Solar Plexus chakra. This chakra has vibrational resonance with the colour yellow.

Heart chakra template

What you need

A rose quartz placed centrally over the Heart Chakra (centre of chest). Use four crystals, points outwards to make a cross along the axes of the body. The most useful stones here are green tourmalines, but alternatively, use clear quartz or rose quartz or other pink stone. It is important that if you use tumbled stones you also use clear quartz points to direct the energy outwards away from the centrally placed rose quartz. Another diagonally arranged cross is made at 45 degrees to the first with four outward-pointing smoky quartz crystals. Additionally a herkimer diamond can be placed just below this layout, though this is not obligatory.

What this template can be used for

Balancing and augmenting the heart chakra functions; integration and balance; sense of freedom; discrimination; friendliness; calmness; outward-looking; decision-making; clarity; lung and heart disorders; circulation; emotional balance; sense of overwhelming responsibility; over-possessiveness; guilt; self-worth; identifying true value and true needs.

The Heart Chakra is "Anahata" - the "unstruck sound" of Creation's vibration. As central point of the chakras, the heart is the integrating and balancing hub of this energy system. When in balance it creates a sense of wholeness and peace, experienced as love. Anahata allows us to see ourselves as harmoniously placed within the scheme of things. The resonance that is the harmony we feel between ourselves and other people and things is an expression of the Heart Chakra. Where the Solar Plexus absorbs and transforms energy from

Heart chakra template

the environment for the continuation of the Self, the Heart Chakra maintains a dynamic balance between the inner Self and the outer non-Self. We can see this in the function of the organs related to the Heart Chakra: both the heart and the lungs function by alternately expanding and contracting - drawing in and pushing out. Balance and harmony is maintained as long as this pattern of expansion and contraction continues. This equilibrium of opposites is what keeps the flow of life-energy, "prana", moving through the universe.

There is a small chakra below the Anahata, known as the Anandakanda Lotus. It is here that our deepest wishes and desires are said to be found. It is described as an altar in front of a tree which when wished upon, will lead to fulfilment and integration of our true being. If you have a need to access this deepest level of your true nature, place a herkimer diamond just below the main chakra template.

The Heart Chakra is associated with the colour energy of green and also has a strong resonance to pink.

Throat chakra template

Throat chakra template

What you need

In the centre of the sternal notch, a blue stone. Directly below this a stone at the thymus gland - a turquoise, chrysocolla or any other truly turquoise stone. Placed either side of the first stone at the sternal notch, a double-terminated crystal (the type of crystal is not important, though it must be the same on both sides). Beneath the turquoise stone on the thymus, breast bone, place a downward-pointing quartz crystal.

What this template can be used for

Balancing and augmenting the throat chakra; sore throat; stiff neck; colds, thyroid problems; hearing problems; any problems with neck,shoulders,arms and hands; self-expression; communication skills; enlivening the mind; understanding symbols, images, concepts; creativity; states of torpor and hyperactivity.

The Throat Chakra is concerned primarily with communication and so it is linked to the colour blue. Communication is the flow of energy from one source to another using symbolic patterns, such as speech and image. The Throat Chakra gives us the means to transmit our thoughts, ideas and desires in order to change and maintain our relationship with the world. It only takes a dose of laryngitis for us to discover how fundamental language has become in making ourselves understood and getting cooperation from others!

We have developed language by modulating the outbreath via the larynx and mouth to create particular vibrations of air, but this is only the coarsest, least subtle, most ordinary level of speech.

In many cultures speech, and particularly the naming of things, is seen as a magically powerful act. What can be named can be understood and perhaps then, controlled. This is as true on the subtle, magical levels as it is one the everyday levels. If you do not know the name of an object you want, it can be extremely difficult to procure it on the physical plane: (a "watchermacallit" or "thingemybob", although expressive is not explicit enough to get you far in a supermarket). Names of power and names of spirits are powerful because of the accuracy, the resonance, the entrainment, that their spoken sound creates in the universe. Entrainment is when a particular vibration sets up an equal, equivalent vibration in its surroundings. Correctly intoning a name of power, or a mantra, for example, sets up an entrained resonance which, at some level of reality creates the object of invocation itself. The difference between the subtle levels of speech and the ordinary levels of speech is the degree of entrainment. In order for a complete energy resonance the name/sound must encapsulate completely and in detail all aspects of that thing - but this sound may not have any obvious meaning in the ordinary levels of thought and speech and has little to do with known language.

The sanskrit name for the Throat Chakra is "Visuddha" which is translated as "pure" or "purification". This chakra functions by purifying, refining or honing out thoughts and desires to create the maximum degree of entrainment possible, and therefore the best chances of fulfilling our desires. The "purer" the sound of our thoughts, the greater energy they have because the closer they are to the true nature of our desires.

Brow chakra template

What you need

Centrally placed on the forehead either a herkimer diamond or lapis lazuli. To either side of this place a fluorite crystal (colour is not important here), and a third placed above the central stone. As an option a blue or violet fluorite can be placed at the crown of the head.

What this template can be used for

Balancing and augmenting the Brow Chakra; eye problems; headaches; mental clarity; "seeing" an all levels; increased perception; imagination; enthusiasm; understanding;intuition.

The Brow Chakra, also commonly called the Third Eye, is the "Ajna", meaning "to know, perceive and command". It is concerned with the understanding and analysis of reality. The Ajna Chakra makes sense of the data received from the physical eyes and the senses. It is also able to go beyond our everyday concepts of time and space to receive images and information from the past and the future - as in memory and in planning future events. As our view of reality is an expression of who we are and how we see ourselves in relation to the universe, the Brow Chakra is the centre where our personality is integrated. We usually experience ourselves as being "in" our heads because we are constantly focussed in the Ajna, projecting ourselves into our future - what we reckon will happen next or what we plan to do if such-and-such happens. It is one of the functions of the Brow Chakra to escape from the constraints of time and space in this way, in order to gain greater insight.

Brow chakra template

However, the danger comes when the chakra loses its balance with the rest of the chakra system and the mind retreats from reality into fantasy and delusion. Then, while we may experience visions, messages and all sorts of psychic information, we will never know what is valid and what is purely wish-fulfilment or worse. The indigo depths of this chakra are profound and inviting but without a balanced and equal emphasis on the grounding reality of the base, second and solar plexus chakras, we can float off into the blue with no compass and no anchors, no use to man, beast or spirit. The chakra template will help to balance the expansive, intuitive functions of the mind within the context of the whole being.

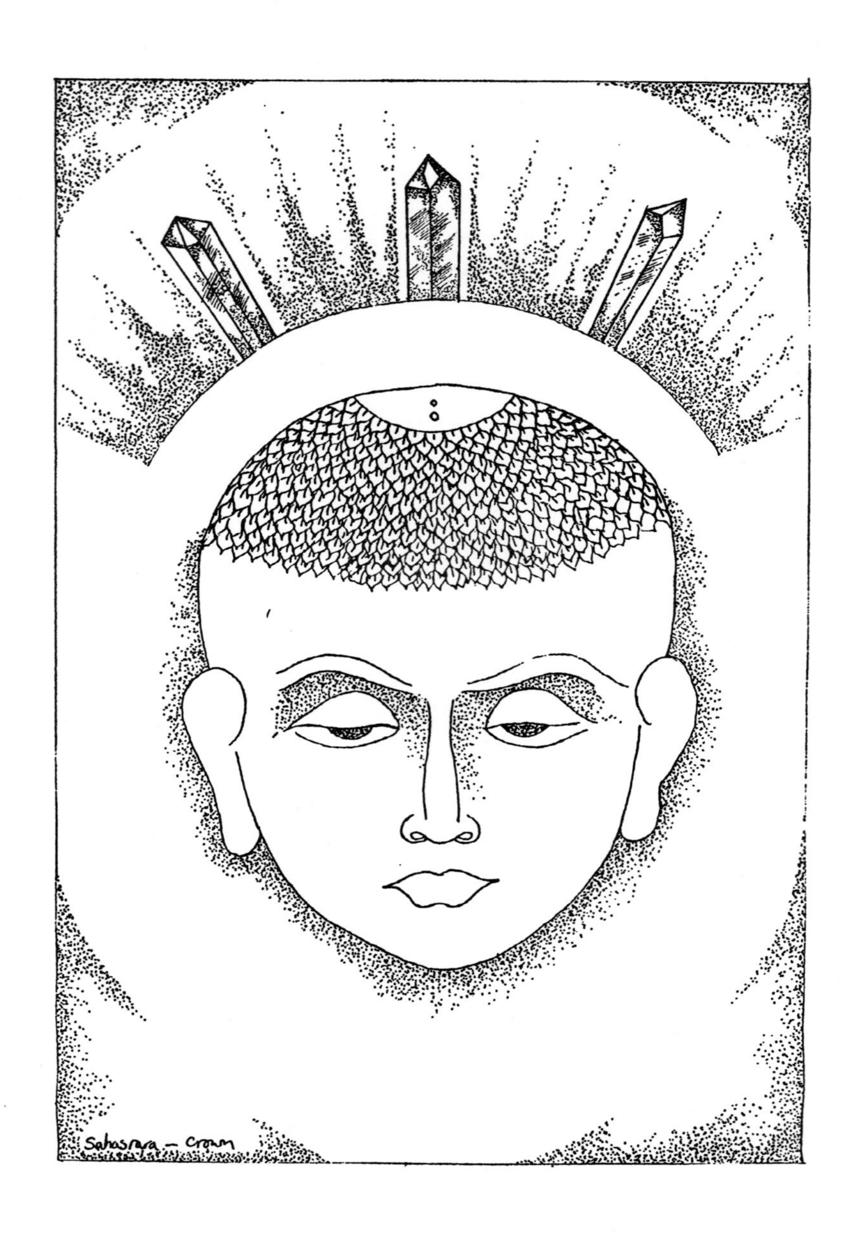

Crown chakra template

Crown chakra template

What you need

Three clear quartz crystals pointing outwards around the top of the head, one centrally placed, the others either side. Other stones can be added wherever it is felt necessary and best to muscle-test or dowse for appropriateness.

What this template can be used for

Increase of understanding and bliss; helps relieve confusion, depression, boredom, feelings of alienation; left/right hemisphere balance and therefore coordination, mentally and physically; increased sense of fulfilment; increased energy and vitality; linking to subtle sources of energy.

The Crown Chakra is called "Sahasrara" - "thousand", referring to the thousand-petaled lotus this chakra is shown as in classical Indian texts. Its location is said to be four finger-breadths above the crown of the head and in some texts it is linked to the pineal or the pituitary glands. The Crown Chakra is the organising principal of the chakra system. Within it is said to exist a replica of all the other chakras and the total pattern of the individual. In this way it is like a projection point from which we are holographically formed, the energetic blueprint which receives and processes all information from the outer universe and from the subtle levels of spiritual energy.

The Crown Chakra is our connection to everything that is. That "everything" is then transformed, filtered and utilised by the rest of the chakra system so that in truth we become a personal lens for the experience of creation by itself. The Crown Chakra is the seat of "knowing" where we can launch ourselves into an infinite expanse of energy and consciousness - it is the place that cements us to the universal power supply.

If we remove the plug we cannot continue to inhabit a body, but if we foolishly open ourselves to greater voltage than we can use, we can blow a great many fuses and end up no better. Developing our awareness is achieved by tuning into the energy of universal consciousness and bit-by-bit assimilating the new energy levels at a natural, easy rate, that the whole of the system is able to adjust to it safely.

Expressing the potential for expansion, completion and fulfilment, the Crown Chakra is connected with the colour violet and sometimes with white or gold. Above the Crown Chakra are another five chakras on the same axis that help integrate even finer levels of energy into the system. Seven is enough for most people to handle at the moment! Once these seven main energy centres become habitually balanced and fully functional, other centres and channels will naturally begin to open as consciousness expands.

Crystal space travel, energy net time machines

We are tuned to the Physical Reality Radio Channel continuously. Our experience and training gives us very few clues to any of the other stations that may exist. The Physical Reality Channel, like any other popular music station, tends to be crude and unsubtle, addressing the perceived primary needs of existence. Like them, it is initially brash and annoying, but before very long any further critical assessment flies out of the window and you find yourself humming along, tapping your feet, alas even singing the inane lyrics of some repetitive ditty, feeling the emotions as if they were your own. Pretty soon it becomes so normal that you may not even notice it, except when, for some reason, it is turned off.

The energy nets, to continue this analogy, are some of the pirate stations available to those willing to take the time to locate them on Reality Radio. The signals may be weaker than you are used to but what they offer can be refreshingly different and may give clues to the possibilities of existence outside the accepted consensus norm.

This book has focussed on accessing some of the primary energy influences that affect us - the Elements, the planets, Master colours and so on. The Element nets cover the foundations of physical matter and its qualities; the planetary nets take our awareness to the other energy "organs" of our solar system and how they characterise aspects of our behaviour and perception; the Master colour nets extend the categorisation of energy influences through from the personal out to the solar system and beyond to the greater universe. This allows quite a range of input (or "radio stations"), to tune into - particularly as each net can be focussed quite tightly by the intent of the "netter" to explore specific aspects. In the

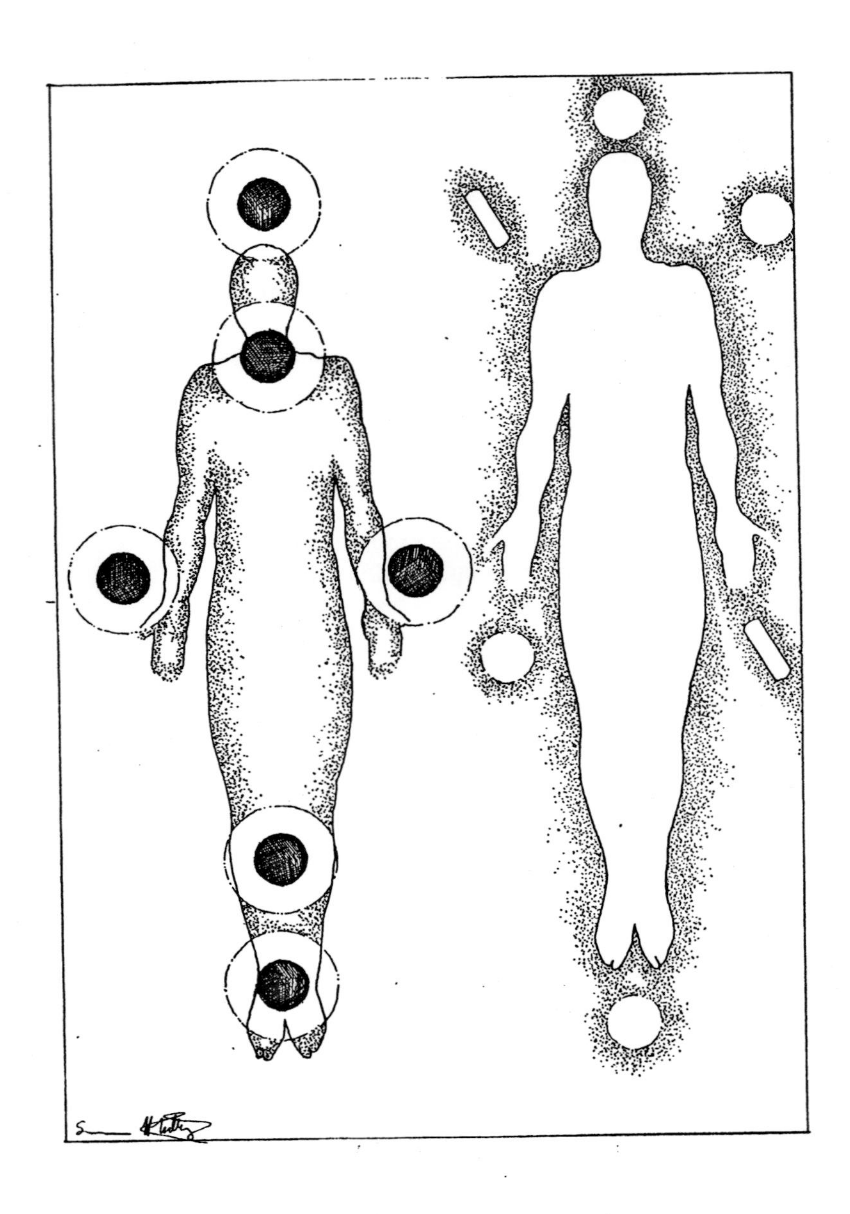

"Space Ships": left: Etheric Body, right: Green Star

ideas and information presented alongside each net there are clues and hints for other avenues of exploration.

It would be possible to go on endlessly discovering new net patterns. Nets for times in history, for cultures, for godforms, for different planes of existence, cabalistic stations, Enochian aethers, stars or even other galaxies. Any such excursion would need considerable planning and preparation, however. The nets we have shown here are those at the heart of our own Earthly energy environment. Unknown regions can pose unknown problems. The unwary tourist "netter" might inadvertently gatecrash another's party. Without knowing the house-rules, there may be, at best, some embarrassing confusions. At worst one might be swatted as unthinkingly as a stray fly or find oneself the surprise course in an exotic menu. There is no instruction manual like the Bardo Thodol or Book of Coming Forth By Day. Unless invited, or with a guide you trust completely, explore territories closer to home.

A crystal energy net is a reconstruction of a certain set of vibrational patterns that we as humans can tune into. It is easy to imagine at a different dimensional scale numerous creator consciousnesses doing basically the same thing, but with larger bits of matter. For crystals see planets, stars, galaxies; for coloured cloth see the background wash of electromagnetic seas in the intergalactic "emptiness" between matter. Set it up, disconnect the phone (as it were), and step inside it to see what happens. Hey presto! another Big Bang.

There are some nets that deal with more than one issue: the Earth net for example tunes to the Element of earth as well as to the Planetary Being of Earth. The Venus net attunes to the spheres of influence of that planet but also can be used to balance the physical level of the body. A "netter" who has worked with us for a couple of years, Nick Skedgel, discovered a net for harmonising and realigning the etheric body - the subtle energy body upon which the physical level relies for its organisation and health. Any diseased state will tend to show in the etheric level before it eventually migrates to the physical, unless it is dealt with here. It can therefore be extremely useful to have a net that will augment the body's healing processes at this level.

The etheric net needs an orange cloth and six carnelians. One carnelian is placed at the throat, one above the top of the head; one at either side at the level of the second chakra, or hara area; two placed on the central axis of the body between the legs - one at midcalf level and one near the ankles.

We came across another net whilst having thoughts,(which may or may not have been our own), on the nature of names, labels and beings. The human preoccupation with superior teachers, deities, Masters, and so forth, of particular forms, might actually block other more useful and appropriate energies from "getting in contact". Labels become so familiar that the things they represent fade into the background. Once the core concept is forgotten it becomes harder to access more appropriate forms of that energy. Also, from the opposite standpoint, everything in creation needs to evolve, to grow. One can imagine the eternal chagrin of some poor deity whose devoted followers keep it stuck doing one sort of redemptive favour or another long after the time when it was looking forward to a change of activity. Gods have ambitions to better themselves as well!

Anyway, the net that arrived at this point was to enable an individual to reach beyond the usual boundaries of energy exchange. It hints at a shift of consciousness to beyond this universe or to looking in a new direction where helpful initiators of growth could be found. This net, shall we call it the "Green Star Net"?, also seems to shift the heart centre into a different dimension. On a black cloth lay out a six-pointed star. The stones, beginning above the head, are chrysoprase; then about sixty degrees clockwise at the second point of the star place another chrysoprase.

The third point of the star is a dark tourmaline; the fourth, below the feet on the body axis, is a chrysoprase; the fifth point, sixty degrees clockwise again, another chrysoprase; the sixth and final point is a second dark tourmaline. The energies experienced are green, comfortable, vegetal, perceptive and definitely unearthly - and bear the stamp of a definite energy personality.

Other examples of nets come from our work investigating the means of interacting with, and learning from, tree spirits and tree teachers. Having first made up a vibrational essence that held the energy signature of a tree species we would work with it to identify other methods to tune into that vibration. Certain sequences of syllables, sequences of colour and musical notes helped to focus awareness, as well as the energy nets using crystals.

In general, the tree nets use less stones and are not so symmetrical, and the "feel" is quite different. For example, the net to attune to the Oak uses a red cloth and all four stones are placed below the feet in a diamond shape.

Immediately below the feet on the central axis is a white or milky opal; below this and further to the left away from the axis is a turquoise; opposite this stone on the right side place a clear selenite (a variety of gypsum), and below these stones in line with the opal, place a haematite.

To attune to the Alder use an orange cloth and place a pink stone of any sort either side of the body, level with the heart. The remaining three stones are placed in a line below the feet. Closest to the body is black tourmaline, then ruby, then milky quartz.

To attune to Yew a magenta cloth is needed. The stones are placed in a curving line up the body. Below the feet a red garnet; beside the left leg, about mid-way, place a purple fluorite. On the second chakra a moonstone; beside the right

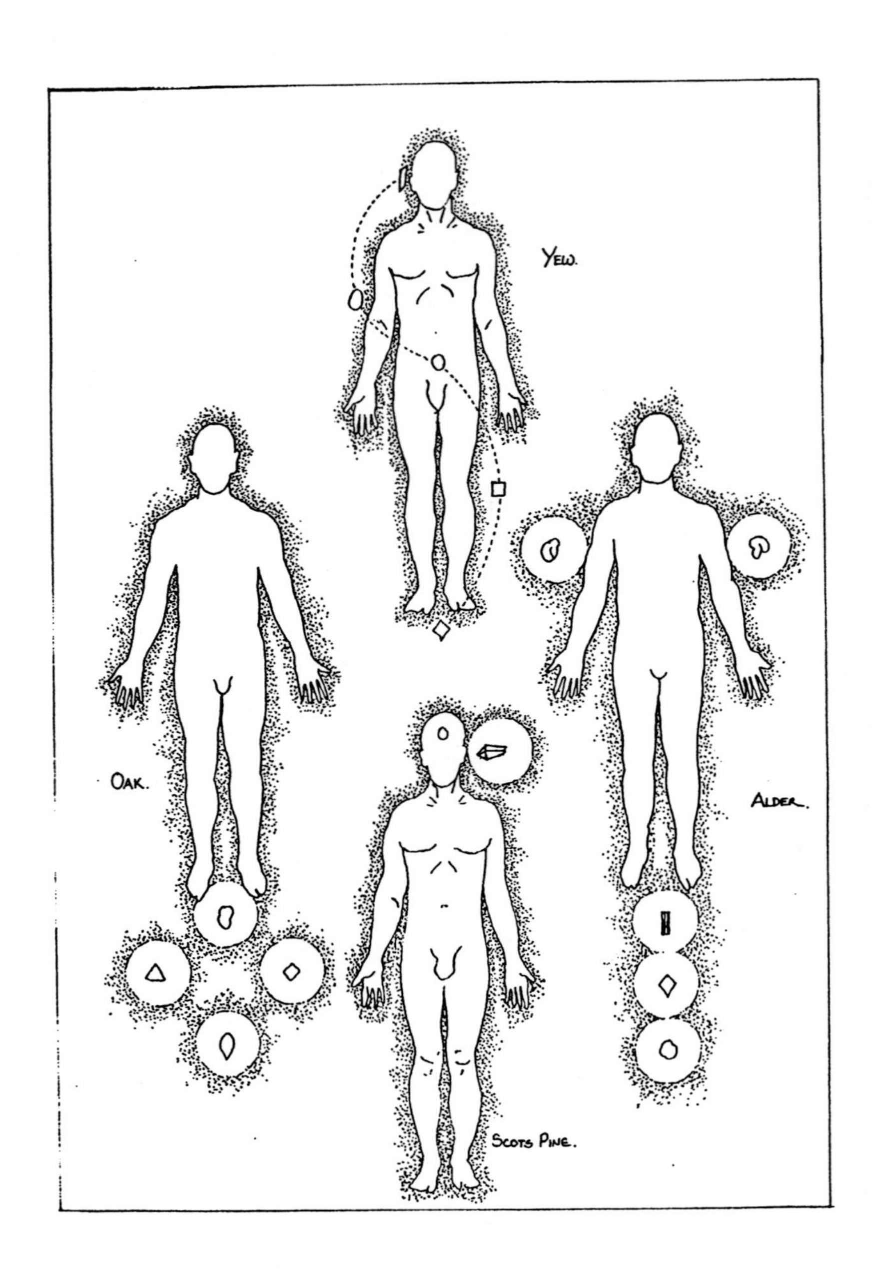

Tree nets

arm, mid-way, a piece of green jade, and in or taped to, the right ear a small, clear selenite crystal.

Some tree nets are very simple. Scots Pine needs a red cloth, a dark blue sapphire placed on the brow chakra and an amethyst crystal pointing in towards the left ear.

If you play around with the energy nets for long enough you are likely to have experiences that stretch your conceptions of time, space and the nature of reality. It is possible to dismiss this new input as an overactive imagination, but is also possible to use the information to construct new paradigms of what is, what is possible and what may have been going on all along without us noticing.

It is really time now for humankind to begin to listen again to what other songs are being sung all around us in the universe. To shut up and learn from the whispers of possibility constantly echoing around us. Energy nets give a chance to tune out of the urban - work - mentality - consciousness whilst we are not asleep. Few of us close our eyes, relax and quiet our mental chatter unless we are just about to drop off into the night's sleep. Even then most of us only crawl to bed when we are already too tired to enjoy the process of slipping from level to level of relaxation and letting go of everyday patterning: of catching the elusive shoals of inspiration that dart through the deeper levels in the ocean of Self-consciousness. This is not only a shame, as we miss the enjoyment of exploration, but it is a great loss to humankind as a species. It is in these quiet, rambling moments that novel solutions, new insights, technologies, healing syntheses, life-enhancing affirmations, evolutionary jumps are able to come up to the surface to be acknowledged and acted upon.

Nets can give us the time and space to roam through the hidden corners of our existence. The more we are able to have direct experience of possibilities the less we need to rely on the theories, ideas and "expertise" of others. There are no experts in the exploration of our consciousness. No-one can tell us how or what to experience in the dimensions inside us and once we are more familiar with who we are we will be less willing to follow unquestioningly received "truths".

The limbic system is a little known region of the brain. Look it up in most books on physiology and it will be passed over in a few vague lines. We were chatting to the Hilarion energy one day (as it were) and the following information built up an intriguing picture:

The limbic node is the key to colour interpretation and translation. This ancient part of the brain links the energy vibration to the colour interpretation.

The base of the skull has a link with the "psychic gate", and the spinal column is closely associated with the activity of the chakras outside time and space. There is an overlapping of function between the chakras and the limbic node. That part of the brain connects the knowledge received through the chakras to the physical, time-based consciousness. Through the limbic system the Being Outside of Time is connected to the Sources. The limbic system is the receiver that can be tuned by colour and also by sound.

Each of the chakras is linked by a system that is even finer than the nadis, to the limbic node - like a superfine version of the spinal cord.

The ability to release information without the time-space limitations could be called time travel. It is a system that bypasses normal awareness. In the same way that black holes and quasars alter time-space, so activating the limbic system gives unlimited access to the finest levels of form. It allows for cognition of any area within the whole.

By training the mind along a wavelength of colour that is fully specific for, and precisely linked with, the wavelength of sound, or combination of sound and notes, the conscious perceptions can be aligned needle-fine, for an infinite distance.

The full clarity of this perception makes the distinction between physical presence and non-physical presence insignificant.

What to make of this? Science fiction material, gobbledegook or hints at a new technology of consciousness? The work of Robert A. Monroe on Out-of-the-Body experiences is perhaps the most scientifically controlled and validated of all "paranormal" investigations and yet it too suggests the nature of reality to be vastly different from conscious opinions. Perhaps after all, as magicians and mystics continue to tell us, there is nothing ordinary about reality. The Universe is Extraordinary. It is about time we began to experience at first hand the subversive nature of Life.

Appendix one

Colour	World	Physical (Body parts)	Physical (Body function)	Emotional
Red	Earth Money Business Practicality	Hips, Legs Feet Coccyx Gonads	Movement Energy Survival	Passion Anger Enthusiasm
Orange	Art Healing Music	Abdomen Kidneys Sacrum Energy blocks Gonads I.C.Valve	Detoxification Elimination Energy flow	Creativity Stress release
Yellow	Information Technology	Kidneys Lumbar	Elimination Nervous systems	Fear, worry Anxiety, panic
	Law	Stomach	Immune system	Joy, happiness
	Learning	Liver Gallbladder S.Intestine Spleen	Digestion	Contentment
Green	Nature Money Power	Diaphragm Heart Lungs Skeleton Thoracics	Respiration Growth	Freedom,control Independence, Duty, sharing Responsibility Love, caring Rebellion,
Turquoise	Communication Healing	Thymus	Immune system Individuality	Self-expression

Colour	Mental	Spiritual/ Cosmic	Essential Oils/Herbs	Crystals
Red	Assertiveness Innovation Grounded Contact with the Earth and physical body	Protection Practicality	Clove, Ylang Ylang Ginseng Patchouli Mandrake	Ruby, garnet Jasper iron Iron pyrites Tourmaline smoky quartz
Orange	Practical art Creativity Practical ideas	Etheric body Cleansing of subtle energies Healing Wisdom	Cedar Mandarin Sandalwood Orange Neroli Tangerine Petitgrain	Carnelian Herkimer Diamond Topaz Citrine Amber
Yellow	Logical thought Memory Discrimination Decision making	Knowledge of Self	Juniper Grapefruit Melissa Chamomile, Lemongrass Citronella Lemon	Citrine Yellow Fluorite Rutilated Quartz Tiger's Eye
Green	New ideas, Old ideas presented in a new way.	Knowledge of boundaries and other realities, Own Path	Bergamot Rosemary Lavender Eucalyptus Cypress Pine Thyme Cajeput	Aventurine Chrysoprase Malachite Tourmaline
Turquoise	Self-understanding Self acceptance healing	Integrated healing Mind/emotion	Larimar	Turquoise Chrysocolla

Colour Mental Spiritual/ Cosmic Essential Oils/Herbs Crystals

Colour	World	Physical (Body parts)	Physical (Body function)	Emotional
Blue	Communication Teaching Nursing Service	Throat Thyroid Parathyroid Cervical Ears, nose	Communication Expression Metabolism Senses	Detachment Loyalty Undemonstrative
Indigo	Forehead	Eyes, pineal Perception Pituitary TMJ	Sight, Compassion Observation	Aloof
Violet	Poetry Art Music	Head, pineal Pituitary Cranium	Coordination Integration Understanding Healing	Sympathy Suffering Sacrifice Brain
Pink	Acceptance	Gonads Tolerance Sympathy	Connectedness Brain	Self-love, Self-image etc... Awareness
White	Brightness	Cleansing Kinetic energy	Perfection, Separateness	
Black	Darkness	Secretive		Hidden Potential

Blue	Clarity Philosophy Learning Intuition	Clairvoyance, audience/ sentience Inner knowing Channelling	Lavender, Rosemary, Clary Sage, Benzoin, Lavender	Blue lace agate Celestite Lapis lazuli Arnica Azurite Sodalite
Indigo	Inspiration Imagination	Co-creator of personal reality	Lavender Sage, Peppermint	Amethyst Sugilite
Violet	Illusion Delusion	Meditation	Violet	Iolite
Pink	Empathy Healing	Understanding of workings of the Universe	Rose, Geranium	Rose Quartz Rhodonite hodochrosite
White	Perfection	Abrupt, visible change	Gardenia Peppermint	Clear quartz Apophyllite Selenite
Black	Subconscious Unconscious Shadow Self	Dormancy whilst change occurs	Obsidian,	schorl Smoky quartz
Multi Coloured			Jasmine Frankincense	Opal Chalcopyrite

Appendix two

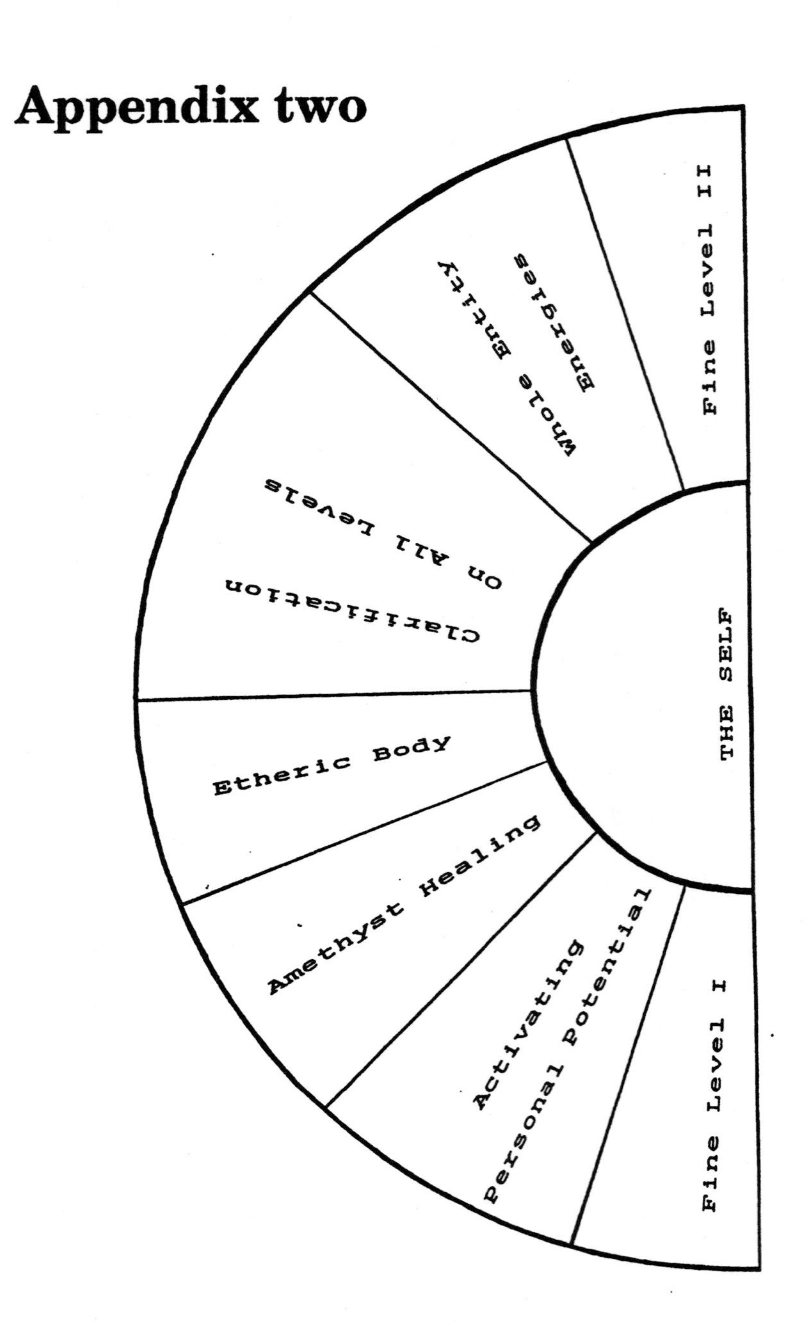

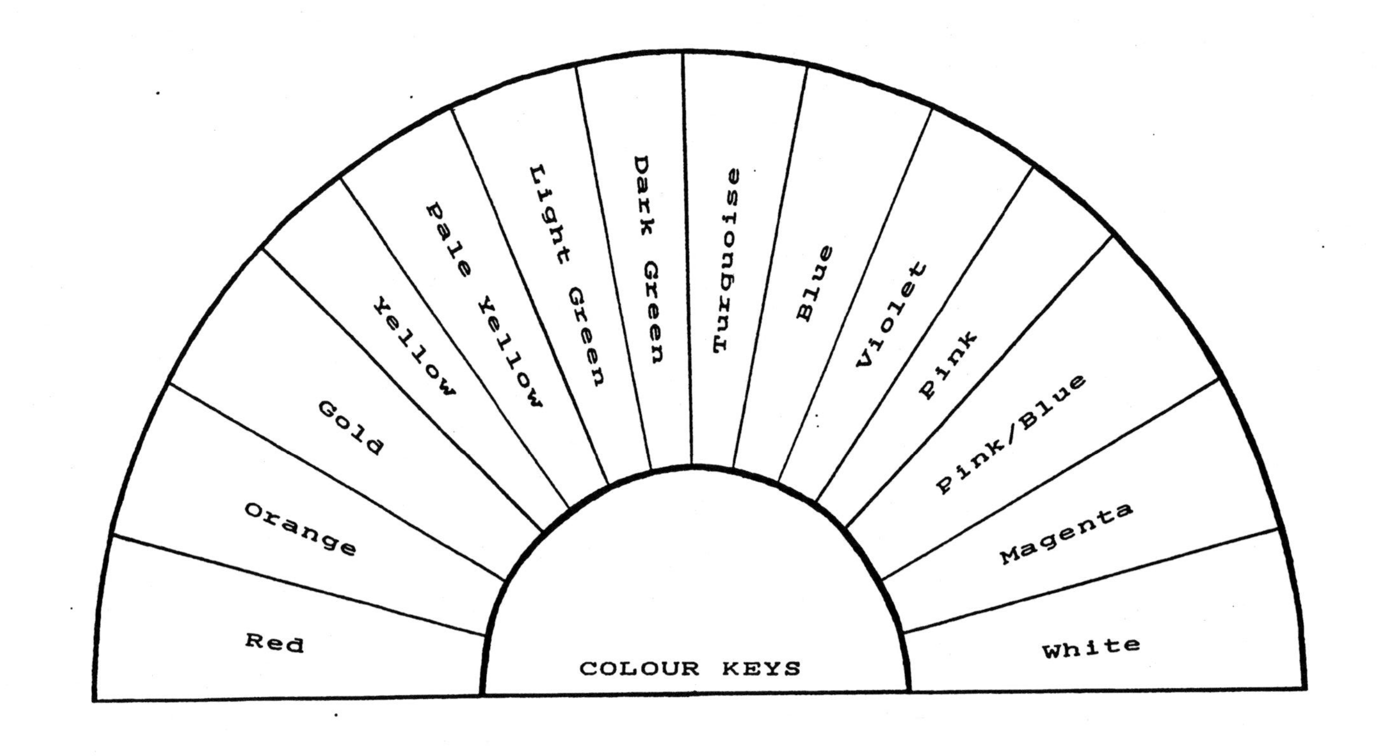
COLOUR KEYS
Red
Orange
Gold
Yellow
Pale Yellow
Light Green
Dark Green
Turquoise
Blue
Violet
Pink
Pink/Blue
Magenta
White

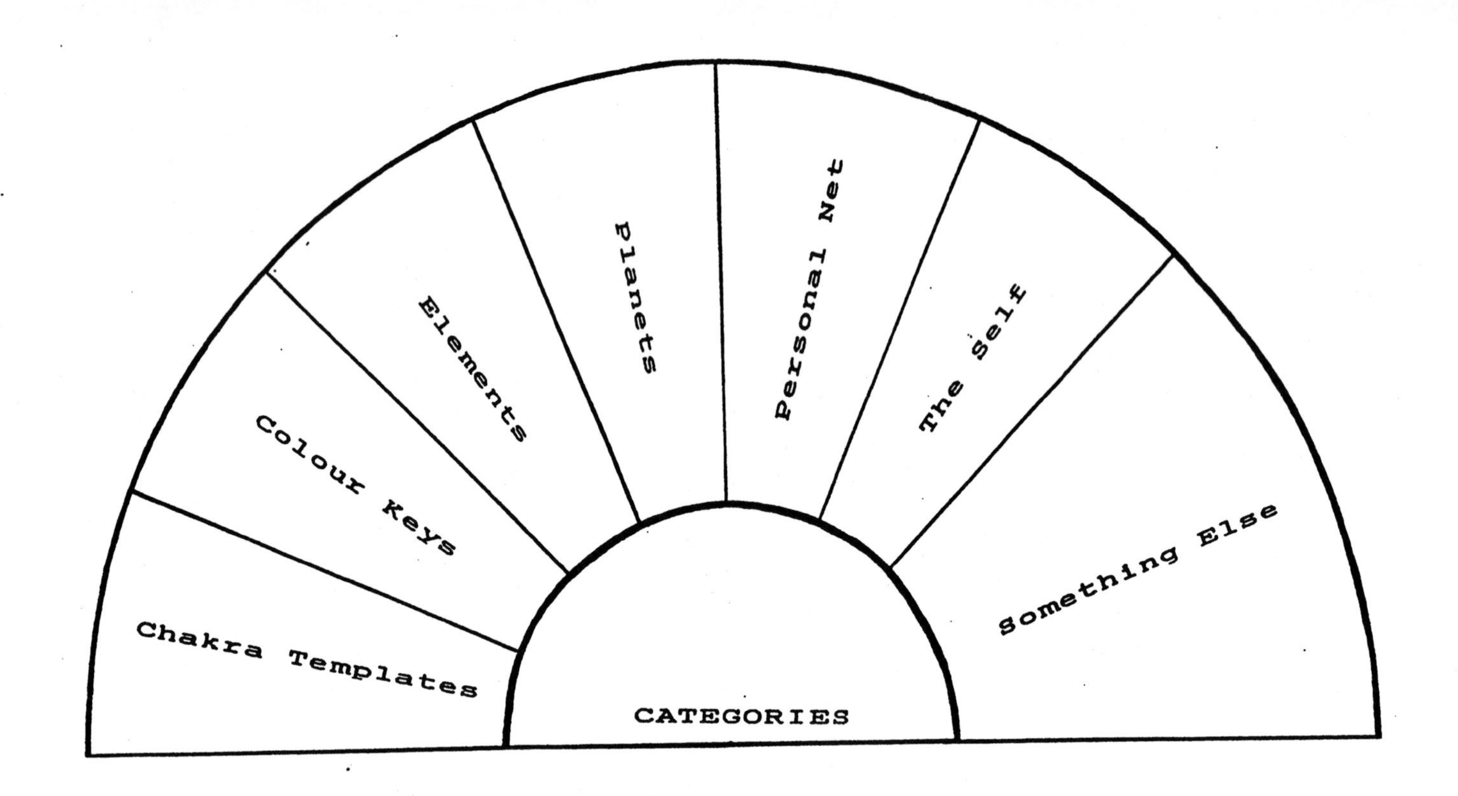
CATEGORIES
Chakra Templates
Colour Keys
Elements
Planets
Personal Net
The Self
Something Else

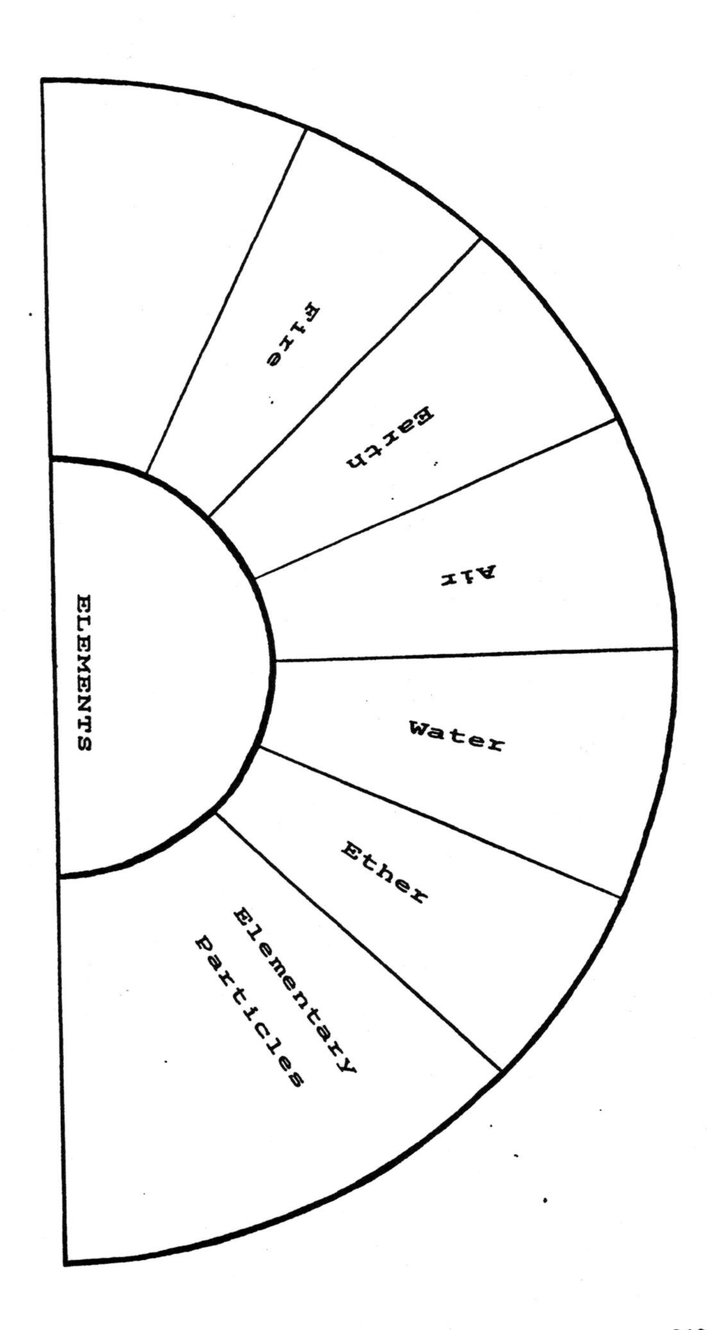
ELEMENTS
Fire
Earth
Air
Water
Ether
Elementary
particles

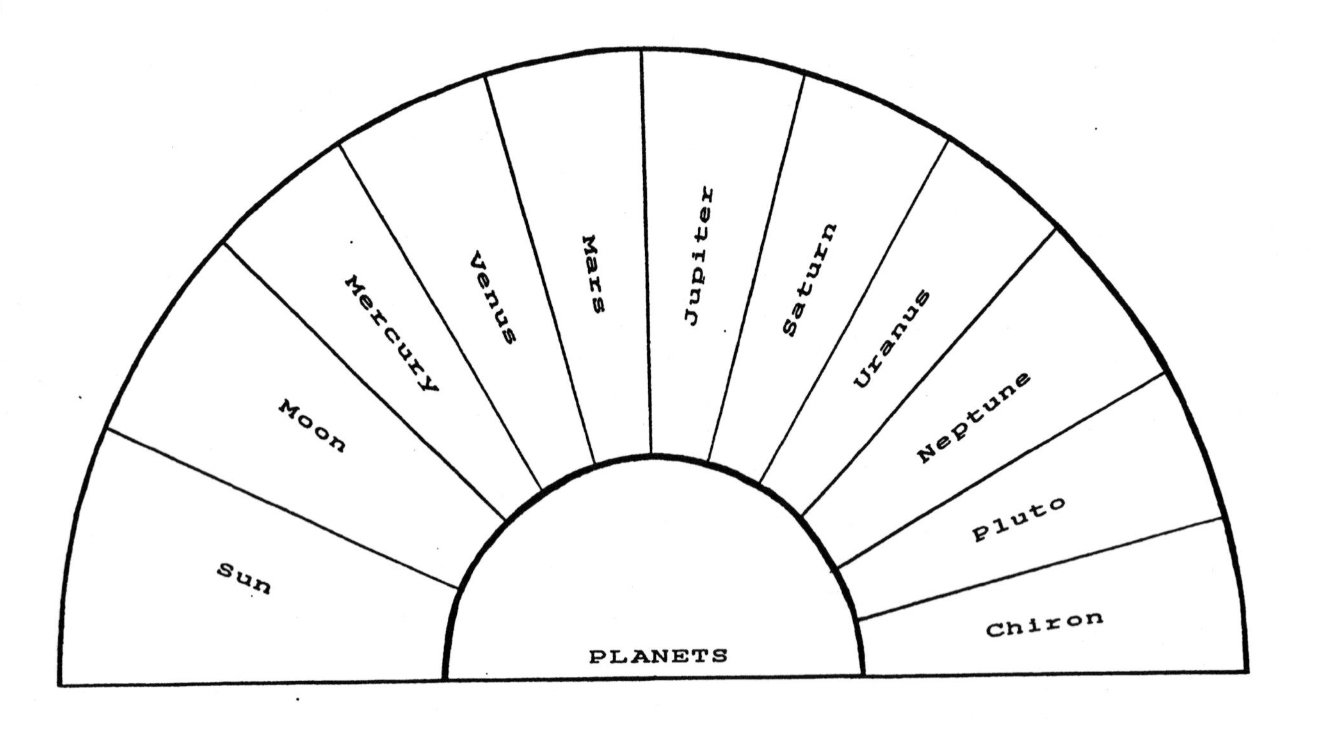
Sun
Moon
Mercury
Venus
Mars
Jupiter
Saturn
Uranus
Neptune
Pluto
Chiron
PLANETS

Appendix three

Step by step guide to dowsing with arcs and to self-testing with kinesiology.

Prior to either dowsing or using kinesiology techniques for self-testing, it is important to establish a firm personal energy foundation.

If your personal energies are disparate, then responses from a pendulum or self-testing will tend to be unreliable.

The following technique helps to establish a secure energy "base-line" which for most people will last for about twenty minutes.

Tapping-In

This can be done by yourself, on yourself, or can be done on someone else to establish their energy base-line.

1. With either hand, bring your fingers together so that the finger-tips are overlapping.

2. Beginning midway down the sternum (centre of chest), tap you fingers onto the ribcage and upper chest at small intervals (about three centimetres apart) in an anticlockwise circle of about forty centimetres diameter. (Anticlockwise when looking down onto your chest.)

3. When you reach your starting point, continue down onto the abdomen, creating a clockwise circle around the navel, and returning to the centre of the chest. This creates a figure of eight (see diagram).

4. Do this 15-18 times.

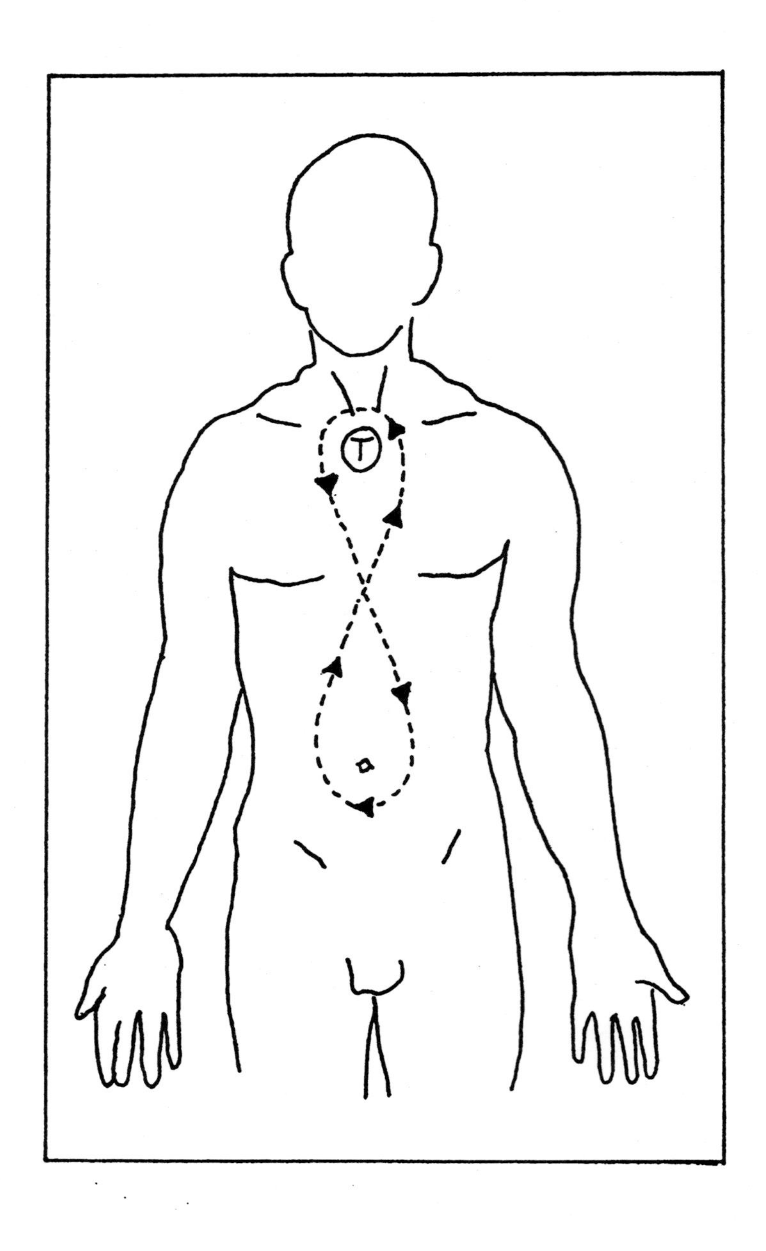

Fig.A - "Tapping-In"

Dowsing

Many people have reservations around dowsing, suspecting that the pendulum can be influenced by the user.

You CAN affect a pendulum that you or someone else is using.

The pendulum represents an extension of your inner senses and amplifies and creates a visual representation of inner energy changes that are occurring. You and others can therefore influence its movement. This tendency can be reduced by "tapping in" and maintaining a level of open curiosity in the mind. Dowsing when emotionally charged or when there is personal investment in the answer may not be reliable.

1. Acquire a pendulum of some sort - a bead on a thread is fine. It is probably best in the beginning not to use personal jewellry, or a needle and thread. The former because it tends to be heavily imbued by the energies of the wearer and the latter because needles can be too lightweight.

2. Draw the figures on the following page on a large piece of paper.

3. Holding the pendulum thread between thumb and forefinger, with your arm bent and wrist relaxed, carry out the following exercises:

A) Over Figure 1, set the pendulum in motion in a straight line away from you. Allow it to swing back and fro for about 6-8 times to get used to the feel. Stop the pendulum with your free hand.

B) Over Figure 2, repeat exercise A, but after 6-8 swings allow (intend, think it, mentally suggest, ask...) the

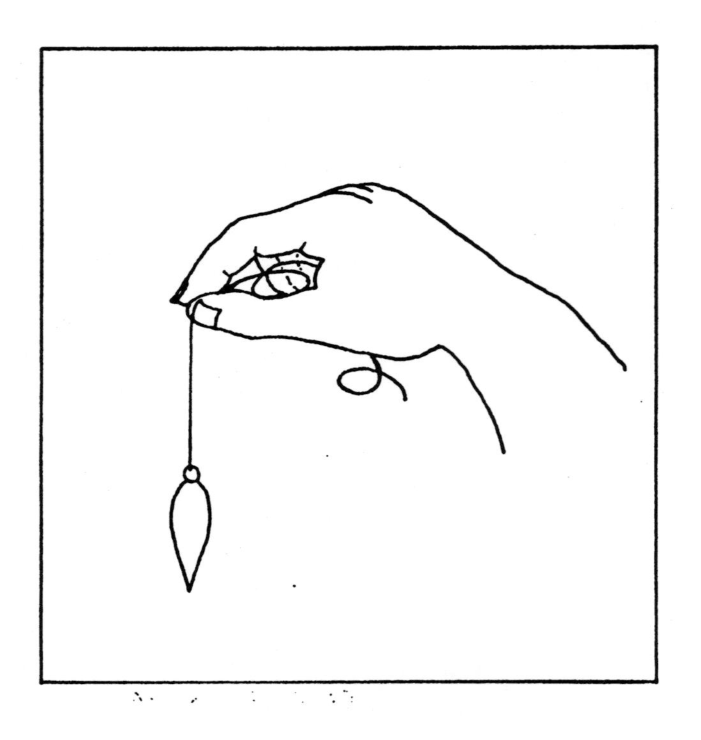

Fig.A Holding a pendulum

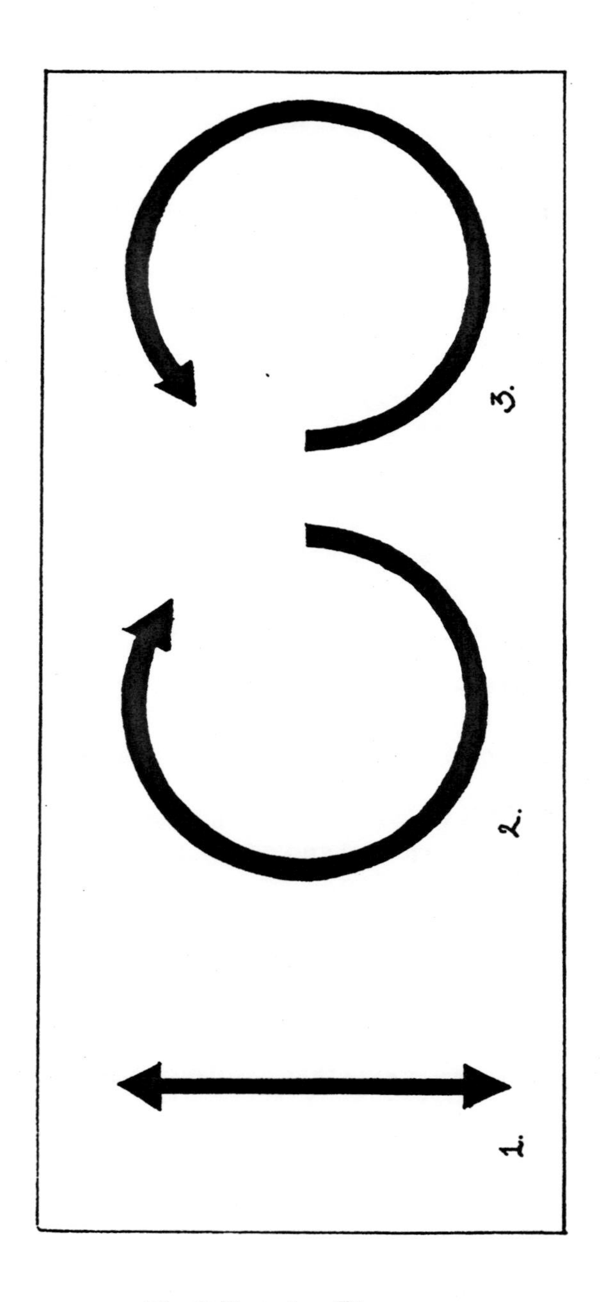

Fig.B Dowsing Figures

pendulum swing to develop into a clockwise, circular or elliptic motion for 6-8 rotations. Stop the pendulum with your free hand.

C) Repeat exercise B) over Figure 3, for the anticlockwise swing.

D) When you are confident with exercises A-C, instead of stopping the pendulum with your free hand, try stopping the pendulum by mental request or intention.

All these exercises help you to become familiar with the pendulum movement and to appreciate how easily you can influence the pendulum swings.

Next step

1. Tap yourself in, using the technique described earlier.

2. With your free hand over your Solar Plexus (between bottom of ribcage and navel), set the pendulum in motion on a straight line swing.

3. Without looking at the pendulum and with an unfocussed gaze, ask to be shown a "Yes" response.

4. After 5-10 seconds observe the pendulum and record the type of swing that has developed. Stop the pendulum.

5. Repeat 2, and ask to be shown a "No" response.

6. After 5-10 seconds observe the pendulum and record the type of swing that has developed. Stop the pendulum.

This process may need to be repeated until you are confident with the responses.

Yes/No responses are very individual - some people have circular swings, some elliptic, some directional straight lines. You need to discover what is right for you.

Using arcs

A few dowsing arcs are provided in the book to help you to discover appropriate nets for use.

Each arc is presented on a sheet.

1. Tap yourself in.

2. Place the sheet in front of you on a flat surface and set the pendulum in motion in a straight line away from you, across the arc.

3. Mentally request to be shown the net that is most appropriate at this time.

4. The swing on the pendulum will then change to indicate the segment of the arc that is appropriate. You can check and isolate the segment by placing a finger from the free hand on the segment, and employing the Yes/No procedure.

2. Self-testing using kinesiology

1. Tap yourself in

2. The left hand - allow the tips of both thumb and little finger to touch.

3. Insert the thumb and forefinger of the right hand, (tips touching) into the gap between the palm of the left hand and the thumb and little finger of the left hand.

4. By parting the thumb and forefinger of the right hand forcibly outwards to contact the thumb and little finger of the left hand, you can test the muscles holding the left-hand finger tips together.

5. If the finger tips of the left hand stay in contact or move slightly and then lock, the energy is still flowing through the muscles and for most people this indicates a "yes" response.

6. If the finger tips of the left hand part appreciably, the muscles have weakened, and for most people this is a "no" response.

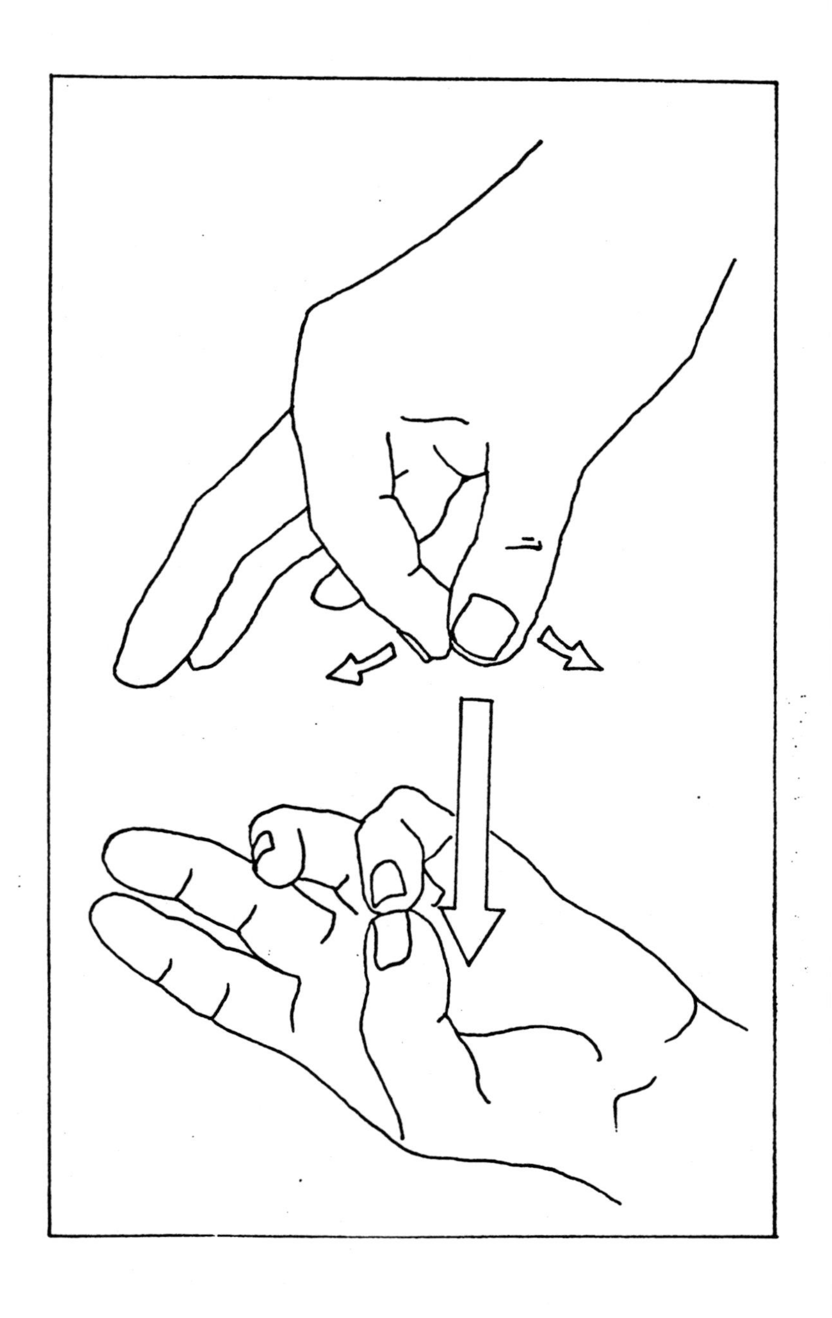

Fig.C - Self-Testing

Appendix four

Astrological correspondences

SIGN	HOUSE	PLANET	CRYSTALS
ARIES	First	Mars	Carnelian, bloodstone, ruby, coral, iron, haematite
TAURUS	Second	Venus	Tourmaline, tiger's eye, topaz, cherry opal, rose quartz, lapis lazuli
GEMINI	Third	Mercury	Aquamarine, calcite, citrine, selenite chrysocolla, agate
CANCER	Fourth	Moon	Moonstone, pearl, amber, green tourmaline, ruby, emerald
LEO	Fifth	Sun	Ruby, heliodor, topaz, sunstone emerald, cat's eye, turquoise
VIRGO	Sixth	Mercury Chiron	Sapphire, peridot, sodalite, rutilated quartz, unakite
LIBRA	Seventh	Venus Some asteroids	Opal, lapis lazuli, emerald, jade aventurine, topaz
SCORPIO	Eighth	Pluto Mars	Turquoise, dark opal, obsidian, smoky quartz, herkimer diamond, ruby, topaz

SAGITTARIUS	Ninth	Jupiter	Amethyst, malachite, flint,blue lace agate, hessonite garnet
CAPRICORN	Tenth	Saturn	Jet, black onyx, rhodolite garnet, clear quartz, schorl
AQUARIUS	Eleventh	Uranus	Amethyst, ulexite, sapphire, jade
		Saturn	chalcedony
PISCES	Twelfth	Neptune	Turquoise, pearl, rose quartz
		Jupiter	celestite

Appendix five

Grounding, earthing, protecting

There are basically two types of techniques discussed here: mentally passive and mentally active. The passive techniques require little mental focus and are excellent in first-aid or emergency situations. Basically, they will work no matter how focussed or unfocussed someone is - it is no use trying to formulate a visualisation or whatever, when you can't tell your base from your crown chakra.

There is little practical difference between the terms "grounding", "earthing" and "protection". If you are fully present in your body, i.e grounded, you are automatically protected from the vast majority of energy intrusions. Likewise, being protected means that the integrity of the body's energy systems is as complete as it can be at that time. You cannot be protected if your energies are flying about at random through different parts of the universe, but this doesn't exclude the possibility of experiencing altered states of awareness whilst remaining grounded and centred. Using the analogy of a tree: only when the roots are firm and secure in the ground can the branches grow up and outwards wherever they like.

Mentally PASSIVE

1. By holding or placing in a pocket or pouch a piece of haematite, black tourmaline or iron pyrites. These tend to focus the body's energy within the physical and help to reconnect the whole being to the Earth.

2. Eating or drinking can help considerably. In emergency a piece of chocolate or other concentrated

source of sugar or quickly digested carbohydrate works by focussing the attention of the autonomic systems of the body by triggering the digestive process. Drinking good quality water can help by activating and balancing the electrical systems of the body.

3. Physical activity, such as walking, running, gardening, stamping, dancing, drumming.

4. Feeling the breath on the roof of the mouth can help calm the mind and the heartbeat and acts to centre the awareness of the body into the core.

5, 6, 7 and 8 come from various forms of kinesiology.

5. Cook's Hook-Up

(Right-handed)

a) Cross your ankles, right ankle over left.

b) Cross your wrists in front of you, right over left where they meet.

c) Twist the wrists so you palms face each other.

d) Interlace your fingers and lay your hands on your lap.

e) Relax, close your eyes, and breathe slowly.

f) When you relax further, release your hands and uncross your ankles.

g) Place your feet flat on the ground and rest your hands in your lap, with your finger tips touching, as if you were holding a small ball between your palms. Hold this for 30 seconds.

If you are left-handed, the left ankle and left wrists are crossed over the right in steps a) and b)

6. Cross-Crawl

There are many ways of creating the energy flow that links each hemisphere of the brain. Any movement where the opposite arm and leg are moved simultaneously will suffice. Here is one example:-

Lifting one knee and touching it with the opposite hand, then repeating with the other knee and other hand can be a gentle, rhythmic way to reconnect the brain. It can also be done with great gusto! Either way it needs to repeated about 20 times.

7. Placing the palm of one hand over the navel and with the other activate either of the following: (You can do one after the other)

a) With the thumb and index finger of your free hand locate the hollows at the top of the sternum, just underneath the clavicles (collar bones). Move the hand so the finger and thumb rotate in tiny circles. These points are at one end of each of the Kidney Meridians, known as the K27's.

b) With the index and second fingers of the free hand, place one finger tip midway between the nose and the top lip (centre) and the other finger tip below the bottom lip, centre, midway to the chin. These are end points to two other meridians, sometimes known as Central or Conception Vessel, and Governing meridians.

8. The "Tapping-In" Procedure outlined in Appendix Three

Mentally ACTIVE

A) Imagining taps at the ends of your feet that you turn and allow excess energy to flow away to the Earth.

B) Imagining yourself under a waterfall, or in the path of water from a fountain. This is both protective and cleansing.

C) Imagining your breath flowing in and out of your feet.

D) Tree Meditation

Begin by relaxing your body into a chair that is comfortable. make sure that your feet are flat on the ground, and that your shoulders are heavy, elbows heavy and your hands resting in your lap.

Take note of your breathing, breathe in deeply and exhale, sinking into the seat.

Take your attention to your imagination. Begin by imagining that roots are growing from your feet, spreading outwards and downwards into the Earth. Feel the nourishment being fed to you, from the Earth.

Feel the energy from the Earth, permeating the lower part of the body, energising it. Allow this feeling to flow upwards through your body.

As it spreads through your arms and trunk, allow it to go upwards through and out of your head. As the energy flows outwards imagine twigs, leaves and branches beginning to appear. Imagine the sunlight beaming down onto the leaves, allowing the leaves to transform the light into energy and food, and be aware of the nutrients flowing downwards into your body.

The energy is flowing upwards from the Earth, through the body, with the energy from the Sun flowing downwards.

Stay with this for a while, feeling your deep connection with the Earth and the Sun.

After a while, focus your attention on the area of the heart where these two flows cross, and feel the stability and security there.

Then, allow the imaginings to fade, but still being aware of the heart then just the breath, and then aware once again of your whole body, especially your feet. Gently bring yourself out of the visualisation.

E) If you are particularly out of it - just do the previous tree meditation focussing only on the roots. Establish roots from your feet and then move up the body, sending roots down into the Earth until you reach the top of your head and roots are reaching down to the Earth from there.

F) Centre-line Breathing

There are many variations to this exercise but the essence is always the same: to focus on a mid-line or central axis of the body and extend that axis up and/or down whilst imagining the breath moving up and down it.

i) Visualise a line through your body from your feet or the base of the spine, up to the top of the head.

ii) Extend that line of energy down into the Earth as deep as possible.

iii) On each breath draw energy up that line into the body.

iv) On each outbreath allow the energy line to extend deeper into the Earth.

v) Continue this for several minutes then take your attention to the upper end of the line. As you draw up the energy from the Earth on the in-breath, breathe it out into the universe through the top of the head.

vi) On the next in-breath, draw the universal energy down into the body and breathe it into the Earth.

vii) Continue this new cycle for a few minutes so that you are alternately breathing in Earth - out to the universe, then in from the universe and out into the Earth.

viii) Don't mind if you find your breathing in and out different from suggested here - the main focus is on the midline in harmony in some way, with the breath.

ix) You can experiment with different patterns of in-and-out breath, but keep relaxed and don't strain to visualise.

IF ALL ELSE FAILS, pain will bring your focus back to the here and now! Icecubes down the back of the neck (or a packet of frozen peas etc.); a cold shower, or if you are really desperate try banging your head against a wall a few times! If you are either a wimp or far too sensible to do this - go to sleep for a while.

Appendix six

God-forms and colour correspondences

RED
Ptah; Khnemu; Rudra; Amitabha; Macha; Mars; Horus; Ares; Christ; Pan

ORANGE
Asklepius; Saraswati; Lao Tsu; Tehuti (Thoth); Ra; The Ribhus; Twashtri; Vishwakarma; Brigid; Kwan Yin; Imhotep; Hygeia; Freya; The Ashwins

PALE YELLOW
St. Francis; Kuthumi; Maitreya; Mercury; Avalokitesvara

RICH YELLOW
Tyr; Maat; Artemis; Shait; Anubis(Anpu); Shamash; Yama; Sammael

GOLD
Brahma; Apollo; Sanat Kumara; Ra; Bel; Belinus; Mimir; Surya; Manjusri

LIGHT GREEN
Laksmi; Kubera: Demeter; Min; Hilarion; Bacchus; Ceres; Isis(Asat); Osiris(Asar); Gaia; Faunus; Dionysus; Cernunnos; Flidais; Gwynn ap Nudd

DARK GREEN
Saturn; Cronos; Djwal Khul; Diana; Vesta; Djinn; Tara; Amoghasiddhi; Raziel; Uriel

TURQUOISE
Viracocha; Oannes; Maha Chohan; Gucumatz; Zeus; Demeter; Quetzalcoatl

BLUE
Chandra; Bast; Morrigu; Gandharvas; El Morya; Jupiter; Odin; Gabriel

VIOLET
Merlin; Ceridwen; Padmasambhava; St. Germain; Circe; Brahmanaspati; Ogma; Taliesin

WHITE
Metatron; Kupala; Juno; Hecate; Serapis Bey; Nerthus; Michael

PINK
Rhea; Anu; Inanna; Devi; Tara; Nada; Haniel

MAGENTA
Artemis; Sekhmet; Anat; Pallas Athene; Astarte; Marduk

PINK/BLUE
Asar and Asat (Osiris and Isis); Khephera; Janus; Ganesh; Orion and Angelica; Heimdall

Elemental correspondences

FIRE
Brigit; Sekhmet; Hestia; Pele; Vesta; Hephaestus; Vulcan; Bel; Agni; Gobnui; Bast; Michael; Djinn; Sandalphon; Paimon; Ohoohotan; Aral; Edlpernaa; Oip-Teaa-Pedoce; Siva

WATER
Tlaloc; Kupala; Viracocha; Nuada; Varuna; Gabriel; Niksa; Thahebyobeaatan; Ariton;Tharsis; Taliahad; Ra Agiosel; Empeh Arsl Gaiol

EARTH
Pachacamac; The Dagda; Seb; Adonis; Pan; Cernunus; Osiris; Cybele; Demeter; Audhumla; Anu; Isis; Uma; Uriel; Ghob; Thahaaotahe; Amaimon; Phorlach; Kerub; Ic-Zod-Heh-Chal; Emor Diall Hectega

AIR
Nut; Arianrhod; Aditi; Neith; Shu; Ashwins; Nwyvre; Raphael; Parald; Tahoeloj; Orions; Chassan Bataivah; Oro Ibah Aozpi

Planetary mantras

SUN	Aum Hrim Hamsa Suriyaye Namah Aum
MOON	Aum Som Somaye Namah Aum
MERCURY	Aum Bum Budhaye Namah Aum
VENUS	Aum Shum Shukraye Namah Aum
MARS	Aum Bhaum Bhaumaye Namah Aum
JUPITER	Aum Brim Brihaspataye Namah Aum
SATURN	Aum Sham Shanaishcharaye Namah Aum

Appendix seven

List of stones

List of stones you will need to do every net in this book;
(Remember small stones are all you need)

Amethyst	8
Aventurine	6 (or other green stones)
Carnelian	6
Celestite	8 points
	7 clusters (small)
Chalk (natural)	16 pieces
Chrysoprase	4
Citrine	3
Fluorite	4
Garnet	4
Herkimer Diamond	1
Lapis Lazuli	7
Moldavite	12
Moonstone	5
Quartz:-	
Clear, pointed	12
Clear, tumbled	5
Clear, clusters	9
Double-terminated	2
Rose, tumbled	12
Smoky, pointed	12
Ruby	6
Sapphire	1
Topaz	2
Tourmaline:-	
Black (schorl)	8
Green (verdelite)	2

Blue (indicolite)	2
Pink/Red (rubellite)	2
Turquoise	6

Others you might find useful: haematite, tiger's eye, jasper, malachite, jade

The following colours of cloth:
Red
Pink - pale
Pink - mid
Pink - magenta
Orange
Yellow - pale
Yellow - mid
Gold/deep yellow
Green
Blue
Purple/Violet
White
Black

If you don't have the appropriate colour for any net, you can use a white background.

Appendix eight - resource list

For supplies of crystals, minerals and gemstones - try your local shops and suppliers first.

Alternatively you can try:

Kernowcraft, Bolingey, Perranporth, Cornwall, TR6 0DH (01872 573888)

Angel, Unit 24-26, The Coliseum, Church Street, Manchester, M4 1PN (0161 702 8191) (Moldavite a speciality)

Everlasting Gems, 46 Lower Green Road, Esher, Surrey, KT10 8HD (0181 398 7252) (Celestite points and clusters a speciality)

If you would like prepared crystal kits for certain nets, then contact the authors for quotes at: 2 Kerswell Cottages, Exminster, Exeter, Devon, EX6 8AY